The
MONEY
in
You!

rayo

An Imprint of
HarperCollinsPublishers

The
MONEY
in
You!

Discover Your
Financial Personality
and Live the Millionaire's Life

Julie Stav

with Gabriel Sandler

To Danny, Tony, Brit, and Jonathan

HarperCollins books may be purchased for educational, business, or sales promotional use. For information, please write: Special Markets Department, HarperCollins Publishers, Inc., 10 East 53rd Street, New York, NY 10022.

FIRST EDITION

Designed by Stephanie Huntwork

Printed on acid-free paper

Library of Congress Cataloging-in-Publication Data
is available upon request.

ISBN 0-06-085490-1

06 07 08 09 10 DIX/RRD 10 9 8 7 6 5 4 3 2 1

CONTENTS

. . . .

ACKNOWLEDGMENTS

. . . .

This book is living proof that the concepts it covers are truly universal. Each one of us who has contributed to making it a reality has brought to the table our own personal traits and our insights on how we relate to money, and in the process of working together, we have grown closer.

My deepest appreciation goes to Melinda Moore, a young woman with a tremendous gift of expression and a depth of character well beyond her years. Thank you, Melinda, for taking care of this baby as if it were your own.

To Rene Alegria, who shared his vision of lustre and jazz to the subject of money and personalities, adding a new and interesting dimension to the text.

To Gabriel Sandler, who from the remote city of Buenos Aires, Argentina, has sealed each chapter with a whispered and intimate final word that captures the essence of my message.

And to you, my reader. I am grateful for your allowing me to feel that my work has helped you realize that your riches are already inside of you.

INTRODUCTION

· · · · · · · · ·

Have you ever wondered why some people seem to make their money multiply like little rabbits while others struggle just to make ends meet? Do you have trouble understanding how your spouse can sleep soundly at night while you toss and turn, worried about money? Where do you find the answers you need to avoid mistakes or, as it happens so often to many of us, find the way out of the money bind you are in?

We all know that financial books deal with just that: financial matters. The good ones can help us understand the financial lingo, teach us moneymaking techniques—when to buy, when to sell. But the story doesn't end there.

Bound up in our relationship to money, we find our personalities, our temperaments, our hopes, our fears, and our self-esteem. In my years as a financial planner, an author of investment books, a teacher, and a TV and radio host of call-in financial shows, I have learned that true and permanent financial freedom is impossible to achieve by addressing only one of these issues at a time. Feelings and finances are inescapably connected.

Even in the stock market, the most successful investors know that fortunes are made and lost primarily due to emotional decisions that are made *en masse*. That's why market pundits have developed psychological indicators to measure the amount of fear, greed, and hope of investors. Have you ever heard of day traders? These market opportunists buy and sell stocks by taking advantage of the emotional momentum that drives a stock price up or down during the course of a day. Their investing decisions are not based on a company's fundamental analysis of earnings per share growth or return on equity. Instead, they sell into the feeding frenzy that occurs when the buzz is created around a certain stock, often discounting whether it has the characteristics that would merit such price increases. Money decisions are uniquely shaped by the personality traits in each one of us, and successful investors have learned to maneuver within their own comfort level. Even the stock market has its own personality!

Introduction

"That's way over my head," you may say. "I just know that all my problems would be solved if I could figure out how to pay next month's rent." Well, guess what? Your immediate problem may be solved when you find the money you need for your rent, but you could find a *permanent* solution to your worries by discovering your personality strengths and how they relate to your financial decisions. If institutional investors and market tycoons acknowledge the importance of the emotional power behind investment decisions, how can we afford to overlook this important factor in our own personal dealings with money?

Mechanical recipes of what to do and not do with our money mean very little unless we are aware of the invisible but powerful forces that propel us either toward or away from our goals. Research has shown that these forces have nothing to do with intelligence, logic, level of education, age, or ethnic origin. Instead, they have everything to do with our behavioral DNA—our personality type.

Each one of us relates to money in a unique way, and when we understand the personal relationship we have with money and how our personal temperament influences us, we are more than halfway on our path to financial freedom. Once we figure out how to bring subliminal money issues to the forefront, we can amplify those that move us closer to our goals and defuse the ones that sabotage our lives.

In this book, I will help you understand the root of your money decisions (or indecisions) by offering you practical tools that will identify your strengths. Once you identify your money personality, use the list of financial alternatives that will work with your natural instincts and cultivate your strengths rather than your weaknesses. Let me show you how to maximize what you already have. After all, why would you insist on writing with your left hand if you were meant to be right-handed?

Tall order, you say? Not really. You may find it in the first chapter, or not until you are well into the book, but the secret key to your golden door lies within the pages of this book—if you are willing to look at the image in the mirror as if you had just met for the first time. I invite you to go on a treasure hunt with me. Together, we will find the magical missing piece to your financial puzzle—the real you!

The
Personalities

1

THE DIVA

Once upon a time, there lived a Diva . . .
Rings from Cartier, dresses by Dior, she dips into her
    coffer,
Always consuming quite eagerly everything they deign
    to offer.
But it could not last, this reign of debt, this tyranny
    of "More!"
Luckily she found this book—salvation is in store. . . .

Jill is a successful advertising executive. Poised and well-read, she has fabulous friends in high places, boundless ambition, and a knack for working a room. Jill navigates her day with the easy confidence of someone who knows her opinion matters.

At the end of a long day, she settled down in the back-seat of the taxi taking her to her studio apartment, and mentally replayed the accomplishments of that afternoon. She closed her eyes and allowed herself to savor the memory of her well-deserved praise following a meeting with the creative department.

The next day's presentation looked very promising indeed. Jill planned to land the largest account ever for her company, and she couldn't help but feel giddy with pride as she imagined the respect and recognition the deal would bring her—not to mention a delightful bonus! Jill's success was a result of the acumen she displayed while assembling her winning team, coupled with her meticulous, yet surely indispensable, supervision. It was hard to believe that it had taken almost two years, but the probable outcome of the next day's presentation would make it all worth it.

As her taxi bumped along the busy commercial streets, an object of exquisite beauty was illuminated against the gray of the cityscape. Jill's eyes opened wide, fixing upon an emaciated mannequin in the highly stylized window of a luxury department store. "Stop, please!" she cried, hurling some money at the confused driver. "I'll get out here!"

As Jill strode across the noisy intersection and closed in on the building, her reflection emerged in the window—appearing to wear that gorgeous designer suit. Jill gasped. Every stitch screamed success, power, and self-assurance—exactly the image she was determined to project in tomorrow's meeting.

Without hesitation, Jill sprinted into the store and straight up to the elegant department where her prize awaited. She ran her nervous fingers through the neatly arranged row of hangers. Yay! They had her size! It was *perfect*! Anna Wintour would bestow her blessings, Coco Chanel herself would coo. . . .

Just as Jill followed the saleslady from the dressing room to the register, a thought fleetingly crossed her mind. The suit was magnificent, envy-making—perhaps the most perfect sartorial creation she had ever beheld, but it *was* incredibly expensive. Last time she had hastily spent that much money, Jill had felt very guilty, almost regretful, when the credit card bill had arrived.

"But I *deserve* it!"

Whoops. Jill panicked; did she say that out loud? A stealthy scan of the room offered none of the baffled or haughty stares that might follow a sudden outburst in this pristine setting. "I work long and hard hours. And besides, my bonus will almost, just about, *kind of* cover it," she rationalized under her breath—to no one in particular. Perhaps it was to her penny-pinching mother, who would be appalled; perhaps it was to the coffee boy, whom she stiffed on a tip every morning; or, even worse, the student-loan officer she had been artfully dodging for years. Jill chose to ignore these nettlesome phantoms, thrust her card over the counter, and, with her Montblanc pen, signed her sentence for the next six years.

Why Our Diva Keeps It All Together

The Diva is determined, dependable, and structured. Professional, educated, with a mind-set geared toward goal achievement, the Diva will be delighted to know that she stands a better-than-excellent chance of succeeding financially if she can manage to rein in her impulsive spending and invest a little time and effort in organizing her finances.

Will the Real Jill Please Stand Up?

Jill may be well dressed, but she's definitely not very well-heeled when it comes to her money. Like many professional women, she has discovered her *earning power*, but not her *money power*. What is the difference? Jill's perfectly

Her Cohorts in Diva-dom Include:

. . . .

Scarlett O'Hara—If she had credit card debt, it would *definitely* be thought about tomorrow. But true to Diva form, she regained control of her fortune and taught Yankee carpetbaggers a thing or two about crossing a formidable corseted woman in the process.

Oscar Wilde—This dandy was forced into bankruptcy for a debt that dare not speak its name, but he managed to always look good, even behind bars.

Judy Garland—This definitive diva died $4 *million* dollars in debt. Divas do tend to overspend on sparkly red shoes.

generous salary demonstrates that she has paid her dues and is swiftly ascending to the apex of her career. But she remains a prisoner of her labor. She is, like most of us, accustomed to having to work for a living, but has yet to discover her money's potential to function as a self-perpetuating machine.

Jill's personality is akin to a freshly laid farm egg. Stable and strong on the outside, but crack it the wrong way, and it can be desperately fragile within. Although none of us falls exclusively under any of the financial personality types I'll be discussing in the book, studies have shown that when we let our guard down and go on automatic pilot in our dealings with money, we tend to follow behavioral patterns set during childhood.

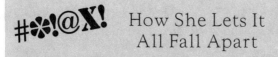

How She Lets It All Fall Apart

The Diva can also be hasty and spend beyond her means if she is depressed or frustrated. Stress and anxiety, while sometimes motivating for this personality type, can seriously sabotage her confidence in areas where she doesn't shine. If money management isn't her forte, the entire issue may be tabled until it's too late.

The motivation behind Jill's extravagance rests in her feelings of entitlement. She *deserved* that suit to fill the void that was left by months of sacrifice, of relentless efforts to succeed without ever taking a breather. It's easy to trace the origins of this line of thinking. Consider the slogans used by successful advertisers: "You deserve a break today . . ." or "It costs a little more, but I'm worth it!"

Whether for chocolate or hair color, a designer handbag or a Caribbean cruise, millions of dollars are spent on research, testing, and promotion by consumer product marketers to attract the kind of emotional spenders who may just be in need of a good night's sleep a great deal more than a quick-fix purchase, which will only temporarily justify their previous deprivation.

The Now

Once money reaches an emotional spender's hands, it's gone, so the first step toward building a nest egg should be to fund it *before* she receives it. Payroll deduction programs, 401(k) retirement savings, and automatic deposits were invented for the Diva.

Since she rarely does things without a purpose, the best way to motivate her to save is by first establishing an ambition for each account. A lavish vacation, a down payment for a new car, or a fancy stereo system can be motivating enough to set this personality type in motion. It's much more exciting to save when you know what you're saving for. The whole point is to reverse the old habit of "spend, pay, spend" with "save, spend, save." By writing down the goal date, the amount to be set aside, and the payoff at the end, the Diva turns savings into an attainable goal and minimizes the chance that those same purchases will be made on the fly—without the funding to back them up.

DIVA-LICIOUS STEPS TO SAVING SUCCESS:

1. Set up a separate savings or investment account. If you mingle it with your regular checking account,

you will almost certainly dip into them and you may
never pay them back. But by creating a separate account for each purpose, you will be constantly, visu-
ally reminded that these funds are earmarked for a
special purpose, and watching the balance grow will
be that much more rewarding and motivating.

2. Decide on a percentage of your gross income or a set
   amount to be deposited into your savings account.

3. Ask your employer if you can start an automatic
   payroll deduction each pay period directly from
   your paycheck into a savings or investment account.
   The old saying "Out of sight, out of mind" applies
   to most of us, and it definitely applies to you. If you
   rely on your discipline to write a check to your savings every time you get paid, you will be tempting
   yourself unnecessarily. No brownie points here—
   this doesn't have to hurt. If your employer does not
   offer payroll deduction, your bank can help. Ask to
   have a set amount transferred from your checking to
   your savings account each pay period.

4. Whenever unexpected money comes your way, put
   some of it into your savings and investments. Bo-
   nuses, salary increases, tax refunds, rebates, and
   overtime pay can add a welcome boost to your account without requiring any additional sacrifice.

5. And finally, if you are forced to dip into this fun account for any emergency, consider it a loan that must
   be paid back within a reasonable period of time. Es-

tablish a scheduled monthly payment, and treat it as one more bill.

Anthropology of a Diva

In my years as a financial planner, when I sat across from this type of spender, the first thing we set out to do was create a spending plan. The Diva's money seems to escape between her fingers, so when I asked my clients how much they were saving each month, the usual answer would be "I don't know where my money goes" or "I don't seem to be able to save" or "I have a good income, but I don't have any money left over at the end of the month."

Since buying is almost an unconscious ritual for the Diva, it is helpful to track spending with no change in behavior for a couple of months. This can be difficult to do based on canceled checks and credit card bills alone. The ATM machine leaves no trace of where the cash goes, and the Diva is apt to make frequent visits to this fairy godmother to make sure her supplies are replenished and handy when the mood strikes.

But by faithfully documenting the money spent—using a small notebook, a PDA, etc.—the senseless cash hemorrhage will become obvious to the intelligent Diva. Many times this is all it takes for her to awaken from her slumber and take the helm of her finances. Once this occurs she'll be ready to plan.

A spending plan—and I would never call it a *budget* when I'm dealing with a Diva, since the word may be interpreted as a limiting measure—should include a set amount each month for prestige items, something she needs to maintain her status and avoid the feeling of deprivation. The difference between this and her former habit is in the planning and frequency of the splurge.

Our Diva is passionate and visionary, and it would be counterproductive to dampen her fiery spirit. If this is your financial type, use your ability to dream big, and to plan big, for optimum results. I'd like to share a formula for goal setting that will help you reach your desired financial destination.

Follow the **Smart** Way to Set a Goal

Specific	Set specific goals that you can clearly name. E.g., save money for a two-week vacation—not just to save money.
Measurable	You must be able to measure your goal. E.g., save $1,000.
Attainable	Make sure your goals are reasonable and can be reached. E.g., you can set aside x amount per month to reach your goal.
Relevant	You must be emotionally committed to your goal. E.g., what benefit will you reap when you reach your goal?
Time-related	Set a definite target date to reach your goal. E.g., "By January 1, I will ..."

Source: Adapted from http://www.pueblo.gsa.gov.

So, let's say that you want to have $5,000 in an emergency account by December of next year. You have a specific amount and a well-defined date to reach your goal. Use the gift of your driven personality to stay the course, but don't set yourself up to fail by relying on your own discipline to save. Utilize your inherent resources; let yourself be charmed by your own cunning!

Consider this: Studies show that when subjects were asked the same financial question posed in two different ways, the results were completely different from each other. These results reveal a lot about how little it can take to switch your mind into a more receptive mode.

One group was asked if they could save 20 percent of their monthly income. The majority of them stated that it would be very difficult, if not completely impossible, for them to do so. However, when the question was rephrased for the second group, who were asked if they could live on 80 percent of their income each month, most of the respondents stated that they believed they could!

Now that you know how to gift wrap the question for your brain, divide the $5,000 you want to save into the eighteen months you have to accomplish your goal—the amount being $278 per month. If you bring home $3,000 a month, $278 represents almost 10 percent of your check. Can you live on 90 percent of your monthly income? If you say yes, move on to the next step by getting in touch with your bank in order to establish an automatic savings account deposit of $278 a month from your payroll department or your checking account. If you are starting to perspire just as you get ready to dial the number, begin with half the amount, but write yourself a memo—I bet you love lists—to make sure you increase it to $278 in three months.

This system may not work with other types of personalities, as you will find out in later chapters, but, Divas, you are the perfect candidates for this program. Your benefit will be measured not only in dollars and cents. If you are stashing some money away for a rainy day, you will be able to revel in one of your favorite highs—the thrill of the spontaneous purchase—*without* the hangover the morning after. Try it—you're going to love it.

The Future

To keep you on a righteous path, you must bring the same enthusiasm for planning you use in your professional life to your financial one.

MAKE A DATE WITH YOURSELF

Since money worries are inherently a part of the Diva's day, designating an evening a week for a planning meeting with yourself allows time for bill paying, reviewing your checking account, opening savings and investment envelopes, and strategizing for the week to come. If you are plagued by pangs of guilt over money, postpone them during the week until "date night."

FIND AN ACCOMPLICE

Divas are usually professionals who are very proficient in delegating work to others. Ask your friends and coworkers for the names of their financial planners and interview them until you find one that complements your personality. Be wary of those who are interested only in the numbers. You must share your spending habits with your planner and not let your need for an occasional splurge get swept under the rug.

The whole point of managing your money is to enjoy financial stability but not at the expense of your emotional well-being. Find a planner who addresses how *you* feel about your investment plan; this is the only way to ensure you will be an active participant in the process. Your meetings will depend on how much your needs change and how comfortable you are with your agent. I remember having clients with whom I met on a monthly basis and others who needed me only once or twice a year to make sure we stayed on course.

The role you play in your work with a planner is to provide the information. Prepare ahead of time by bringing with you a list of your goals, your monthly income, and your regular expenses. Your adviser's role will be to take the wheel and drive you to your desired destination. You know where you want to go; use your planner as a GPS to get you there. But don't relinquish your power. It's *your* money.

Now then, financial planners come in three flavors:

- *Fee-based planners:* This type of counselor charges for their services, either on an hourly basis or a flat fee for meeting with you, gathering your information, and developing a written plan of action. You meet regularly, and afterward your planner should provide you with a detailed summary of your financial situation, including income, fixed expenses, net worth, an inventory of your savings and investment accounts, your financial goals, and the specific recommendations of changes that need to be made in order to meet them. Usually, this type of planner does not help you to implement your program. It would be up to you to find a broker, insurance agent, or another representative to set the plan in motion. Think of this kind of planner as an architect who draws the plans for your new home. You would still

 There is a three-letter title that is used only by Certified Financial Planners—those who have completed a rigorous course and extensive testing. To find a CFP, as they are commonly known, in your area, or for more information, you may visit the Financial Planning Association at http://www.fpanet.org. Prior to any payment, be sure to ask for a written agreement that delineates what is expected from each party and the terms of the payment schedule.

need to find a builder or contractor to execute the plan.

- *Commission-based planners:* These planners don't charge a fee for meeting with you, going over your documents, or helping you set up your goals. They earn money from commissions paid by the different investment companies they represent. Don't worry, you won't save money bypassing the agent and going directly to the investment company; it's much less expensive for the company to pay the commission than it would be to hire more personnel to counsel you and hold your hand through the process. The most important factor to consider when consulting commission-based planners is to find out their criteria for recommending a product to you, and to find out how many investments are represented by the

The most important factor in dealing with any agent is the rapport you can establish with that person and the ethics with which your business is handled. Word-of-mouth referrals and a visit or a call to the National Association of Securities Dealers Regulations (800-289-9999, www.nasdr.com) or the National Association of Insurance Commissioners (816-842-3600, www.naic.org) to inquire about any particular planner can give you some degree of reassurance.

firm. You don't want to be limited to only those that will pay a high commission to the agent. There are independent brokers who represent many companies, and there are captive agents who represent only one. Ask for references.

- *Fee-commission planners:* This type of planner charges a fee for the consultation and then may also make a commission from your investments. In this case, the architect is also the contractor. Sometimes the initial consultation fee is waived if you implement the plan with the same planner.

Are You a Diva?

· · · · · · · · · · · · ·

Here is a simple quiz!

There are no right or wrong answers. You can't fail this test. Give it a try. . . .

Circle your response for each of the following statements:

1. If I received a $50,000 gift, I would probably say to myself: "Wow! Now I can buy something awesome!"

    I agree   I disagree

2. I am so busy making money that I don't have time to manage it.

    I agree   I disagree

3. If a friend asked to borrow money from me, I would feel flattered and probably lend it.

   I agree   I disagree

4. When I find something I like but can't afford, I usually buy it anyway. After all, that's the reason I work.

   I agree   I disagree

5. When I go out to lunch with a friend I enjoy picking up the check.

   I agree   I disagree

If you circled "I agree" for three or more questions, chances are you are a Diva who values the status and power that money can bring you. If you still have your doubts, take a tour through your own closet and see how many items you can find with their tags still attached. Return them. You probably bought them on a whim.

Most of your ilk can take control of their money simply by focusing on doing so. Previously, you've been working for your money so hard that you forgot to put your money to work just as hard for you. Think of your financial plan as the ultimate professional project. When you learn to shift gears in this way, there will be two of you pulling in the same direction.

Your first assignment is to live on 90 percent of the

money you make. After all, why should you wait until the end of the month only to realize that there is no money left over to fund your dreams? You *deserve* to be placed at the head of the line. You have been granted the gift of ambition. Now put your dreams into a realistic time frame and set in motion an automatic pilot so you don't get in your own way. Every time you get paid, claim *your* share from your check directly into your special accounts. After all, *you are worth it!*

A *Final Thought for* . . . *the Diva*

You are a unique and special person. You have skills, styles, and abilities that allow you to enjoy your success today. You have achieved it by yourself. With some help, and despite obstacles, you definitely overcame the challenges and took advantage of the opportunities that came your way.

You learned what had to be learned. You did what had to be done. It was you who spoke up when something needed to be said. Abandon, then, the feeling of insecurity and uncertainty that often torments you and causes that fearful emptiness inside you. Recognize it, be aware that it is approaching, and prepare to confront it with decisiveness and confidence. You become stronger each time you deal with the issues at hand.

You are not the one choosing—on the contrary, you are being chosen. The anguish and anxiety set up a trap, and you allow yourself to become their prey. You will be captive to those feelings and—far from being able to enjoy the result of your decision to be guided by your own instinct—you will feel repentance, guilt, and remorse.

You must be aware that you don't have to impress anyone. An expensive dress, perfume, or fancy new automobile will not help you win anyone over. If you win anyone's respect, it will not be through material goods, but through your attitude, integrity, wisdom, and honesty, and by being faithful to your own values and ideals.

Above all, the one you need to focus on impressing is you—that true being that dwells inside of you. By working toward impressing yourself, you will gain the respect and admiration of those around you almost without realizing it.

The next time you feel that sensation of emptiness, that itch that makes you act impulsively and against your good judgment, stop, take a step back, and look at yourself. Take time to feel, think, and remember that the means to your success are not on the outside, but rather deep inside of you.

2

THE
DO-GOODER

Once Upon a Time, There Lived a Do-Gooder.

So dark in here . . . oops!
Forgot to pay bill. Again.
Let's tell ghost stories!

Tom has been a counselor for a nonprofit social service agency for over ten years. A bit hippie, a little boho, Tom has the soothing demeanor of Mister Rogers and a hearty, contagious laugh. His income is modest, which suits him just fine, as long as he can manage the rent on his smallish digs. He's thought about finding a larger place to live, maybe even in a better neighborhood, but guilt creeps in when he entertains these notions of grandeur. House hunting and notions of upward residential mobility are dismissed out of hand.

One brisk morning, Tom pedaled the mile and a half to work, digging the bright azure sky and the awesome crunch of the snow beneath his bike tires. Even the hypothermia-inducing wind that tore straight through his skin and turned his normally warm, plump hands into freeze-dried pork chops had its own willful charm. Tom took pride in the fact that he didn't need to buy a car or contribute to diminishing the air quality of his city. Even though it was awfully cold out, after climbing one of the hills on the way to his office, Tom had warmed up significantly. With one pork chop gripping the handlebar, he used the other to loosen the alpaca scarf from around his neck in the precision bike ballet he'd perfected over the years.

This morning, however, luck was not on Tom's side, and the scarf flew out of his icy grasp, sailed on the frozen wind, and glided suicidally off a bridge.

Darn. The scarf had been Tom's favorite, a gift from a coworker who'd indulged in a monthlong sojourn in Guatemala. Tom would have to get a new one because it was freezing outside, but he never delighted in shopping, especially for himself. He didn't care much for large department stores or crowded malls; he found them overwhelming and not just a little depressing. It didn't much matter anyway; he had many of the everyday items in his apartment and the clothing in his drawers for years—some since college—and he was willing to take a trip to a flea market or a nearby yard or stoop sale to supplement his supplies.

Grocery shopping was perhaps the only indulgence for Tom. He made frequent purchases at the local organic store a couple of blocks from his apartment, even though he paid a hefty premium for the privilege. But Tom felt good about buying his food this way—knowing he was supporting one of the small businesses in his community, and simultaneously buying quality products free of pesticides, antibiotics, unfair trading practices, and whatever else the heartless industrial agriculture and livestock barons could come up with.

In spite of his modest lifestyle—actually, because of it—Tom had always been a generous contributor at his church and to the charities he so earnestly supported with both his time and his money. Tom had always been a pretty happy, contented guy. He had a job that, although not high in monetary rewards, provided him with the satisfaction that he was doing something to make the world a better place, one person at a time.

He had opened a money market IRA at the local bank a few years earlier, and he had been depositing $50 per month in the account. This, he *guessed,* would bring him an adequate income in his retirement years.

Tom had a coterie of close friends that he'd known for years. One of them, Robert, a coworker with an adventuring spirit, had borrowed from Tom some of the money he used to take the Guatemalan vacation. Robert had returned, smiley and invigorated, but seemingly without explanation about when Tom could expect his money. After a few uncomfortable encounters in the hallway, Tom

Why Our Do-Gooder Keeps It All Together

The Do-Gooder is generous and virtuous, with an inner peace that is fueled by honest work, family, and friends. He is not easily seduced by advertisements or the allure of acquirement. The Do-Gooder is a marvelous candidate for long-term savings plans and will have an easier time than most refraining from the temptation to fiddle with his financial blueprints.

How He Lets It All Fall Apart

The Do-Gooder is careless about money to the point of obfuscation. His trusting nature can make him vulnerable to financial predators, especially when they are disguised in Granny's nightgown (or are, in fact, Granny). The Do-Gooder does not want to be a burden on his loved ones, but if he doesn't make plans for the future, it's a likely outcome.

decided that he wasn't going to press Robert for repayment. After all, their friendship was a lot more important to him than the loss of the money, and who's to say that the cozy alpaca scarf (RIP, scarf . . .) wasn't worth the $300 Tom had handed over to an (at the time) extraordinarily grateful friend? Mutual friends of both men were nothing short of appalled at Robert and had strongly encouraged Tom to demand repayment. Tom wanted nothing more than to keep the peace, and if that meant contentment with a fuzzy scarf as opposed to his plans to use the money to go white-water rafting, so be it.

Will the Real Tom Please Stand Up?

Tom's purpose in life is to be generous with his time, expertise, and contributions in order to serve humankind; he is virtuous indeed. A forgiver and forgetter at heart, there may be a few entities for which, try as he might, he still harbors some disdain. Ralph Nader is one. And the other? The most corrupting, corrosive force on earth?

It's money, honey.

With ample evidentiary support, Do-Gooders can proclaim that money is, and has been, a root cause of much of the evil perpetrated upon humanity. The world's money-mongers are those he respects the least, and, as naturally follows, those whom he most admires are the ones who frequently, almost forcefully, do without. That his future children might one day grow up attempting to emulate a Paris Hilton above a Mother Teresa shakes poor Tom to the core of his being—and he has resolved to take whatever steps necessary to shield himself and his family from the trappings of the gruesome dollar.

Unfortunately, Tom's single-minded correlation of money to misery is blinding him to the security that comes with a well-rounded financial plan. By following his natural instincts to live frugally and be virtuous with what little money he does have, he runs the risk of being overly selfless, and ultimately unable to adequately provide for himself and his loved ones.

If you are reading this book about money, there's a decent chance that you are not a Do-Gooder, since most tend to frequent the financial section of their local indie bookstore about as often as they TiVo *Dynasty*. But we all have people like this in our lives, and for better or worse it is important that at least someone in their sphere of influence can hand over advice.

The Now

Apathy is antithetical to the Do-Gooder, since this kind of hands-off haughtiness, even as it applies to money, does little to change the state of affairs. So, to jump-start Do-Gooders, the best thing to do is link financial well-being with family happiness, charity, and social progressiveness. They will view wealth as important only if the success of their portfolio will help those in need.

Do-Gooders follow their hearts, even in their investment decisions, and luckily, they don't need to neglect "doing good" in the world in order to "do well" for themselves. Socially responsible investing is tailor-made for this type of investor. If the term "socially responsible" evokes images of complacent tree-hugging folks sitting in a circle and singing "Kumbaya," I have great news for you.

Socially responsible investing (also known as SRI) has been around for decades. The most common denominator among these companies is the fact that they not only abide by the rules of the appropriate regulatory agencies, but they also answer to the calling of the greater good. For example, a company may be considered socially conscious if it doesn't support the tobacco, gambling, alcohol, or defense industries. A company may have a great environmental record, defend and demand human rights, support labor issues, or even take a particular stance on abortion, global health, or animal welfare.

One of the SRI formats that people are looking closely at these days centers on researching, supporting, and funding alternative fuel sources—for obvious reasons this is an area that has seen interest spike considerably in the last few years. On a more intimate, yet equally compelling, scale, we find the microfinancing movement, which offers small, low-interest loans to individuals in underdeveloped areas. Microfinancing has caught on rapidly, not only for its nearly flawless record of return, but for making an obvious social impact on the areas where it has gained traction. Many of these loans are made to women and are used to purchase moderately priced entities—livestock, or the building materials to start her own business.

An investor can buy shares of socially responsible companies through a brokerage account, one or more shares at a time, or he may choose to buy shares in a mutual fund that invests in companies with a common social theme.

You may not be surprised to hear that the first socially conscious fund opened in the early 1970s. Yep, right along with psychedelic T-shirts, first-run episodes of *Laugh-In*, and antiwar demonstrations, Pax World Management Corp. launched the first mutual fund that used social as well as financial criteria to choose its investments. Today,

there are over 175 mutual funds that appeal to bo.
hearts and our pockets.

Take a look at the following graph.

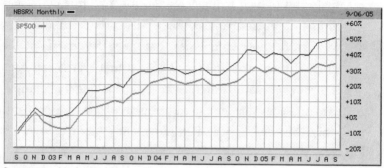

The bottom of the graph indicates the months for the three years from September 2002 through September 2005. The right-hand column represents the percentage of change in share price.

The top line on the graph represents the share price during the three-year period of one of the most profitable socially responsible mutual funds, the Neuberger Berman Socially Responsive Fund (its symbol is NBSRX). The gain over the three years was more than 60 percent, which means that an investment of $1,000 turned into $1,500 over thirty-six months. The line almost parallel to the Neuberger fund represents the growth of the Standard & Poor's 500 Index, which is the share price of five hundred leading companies in the United States that are generally considered to represent the stock market as a whole. During the same period of time, the S&P 500 had an increase of less than 50 percent.

The Neuberger Berman fund, a mid- to large-cap mutual fund (which is finance lingo for investments in medium to large companies), uses a financial screening system to identify those companies that meet the criteria of the fund. It then takes the result of that first search and runs it through its social criteria screening, looking for "companies that show leadership in the areas of the environment, workplace diversity and employment." (Source: www.nb .com)

The Future

KEEP YOUR EYE ON THE BIG PICTURE

Instead of concentrating on a budget or a spending plan for a Do-Gooder, I found it very helpful to engage in conversation about his wishes. Tom may not know how much money he will need on a monthly basis when he retires, but if you ask him what he would like to do for others if he had the money to do it, you'd better be prepared to write and write fast.

Do-Gooders can visualize themselves doing what they love to do, and once they understand the concept of providing for themselves first so they can afford to dedicate their time and energy to helping others, it becomes much easier to establish a savings and investment system. Darling Do-Gooders, put on your oxygen mask first, and *then* assist those around you.

MAKING IT WORK HARD

There are three areas where Tom can maximize his retirement income:

- The first is in his existing IRA account. Rather than keeping the money in the bank, he could transfer this account to a good socially responsible mutual fund that also appeals to his social sensibilities. Tom can Google the term "socially responsible" and have access to the leaders in their specialized fields. I cover the subject of mutual fund selection step by step in my book *Fund Your Future*.
- The second place where Tom can put some money aside and in the process receive assistance from Uncle Sam is in a tax-sheltered annuity program, also known as a 403(b) plan. This type of retirement program is offered by most nonprofit organizations. It works similarly to an individual IRA with the added benefit of offering higher annual deposits and the ability to borrow from your funds should the need arise. Tom's payroll office or the person in charge of human resources can provide him with more information.

- Annuities are very popular with Do-Gooders. Simply stated, an annuity is a savings account with an insurance company. It is not a life insurance policy, and no medical tests are required.

Annuities have many advantages over other types of savings programs. You do not pay taxes on the gains of your account while the money accumulates. If the money sat in a bank, earning interest, at the end of the year you would receive a form 1099INT from your banking institution, alerting you to declare the interest earned during that calendar year in your income tax declaration. You need to file this extra paperwork even if you did not withdraw any money from the account. An annuity, on the other hand, legally shields the interest earned from taxes until you withdraw it. That's why it's called a tax-deferred account—you defer paying taxes on the gains. The result is a substantially larger pot, boosted by the interest on monies that would have otherwise gone to pay taxes. It's a handy way to give your savings extra oomph.

Annuities also carry guarantees, and that is important to a saver who does not wish to risk his money. Most annuities guarantee that they will pay you at least a certain interest on your money; typically this rate is 3 percent. The most vanilla of the annuities is a type called a *fixed annuity*. You deposit your money, either all at once or over a period of time. You earn the current rate of interest (never less than the guaranteed rate the company stated on your contract). How can they guarantee you a return and not put your money at risk? By giving you an incentive *not* to touch your account for a definite period of time. That's right, you need to make a commitment to the company that you will not make any withdrawals from your account for a period of what could be one to fifteen years or longer. That way, the insurance company can also make long-term commitments with *your* money and earn a higher rate, which it will in turn pass on to you.

There is a variation of a fixed annuity, which bases the interest that you receive on the growth of the S&P 500 index. These annuities are called *index annuities*. They appeal to savers who still want guarantees on their money but would also like to participate in the growth of the stock market. The insurance company uses the percentage increase of the index as a base and then pays the accounts a portion of that interest gain. For example, if you had an index annuity that paid you 50 percent of the index gain, and the S&P 500 index grew by 8 percent in a given year, your gain would be 4 percent (half of the market gain).

But some annuities can carry risk. This type of account is called a *variable annuity*. Instead of having your money sit in a savings account, earning interest, the insurance company uses your money to purchase shares in a selection of subaccounts that work like mutual funds. The guarantee of your money is not a built-in feature in variable annuities. Your account value will increase or decrease according to how your chosen funds perform.

- Uncle Sam also has some demands on you if you want to shelter your interest from him. If you withdraw money from an annuity—regardless of the type you choose—before you turn fifty-nine years old, you will not only have to pay taxes on your gains, but you will also be assessed a penalty from the federal government of 10 percent of the amount withdrawn. These accounts were designed to be used for retirement purposes and the magical age, according to the illustrious uncle is 59½, and not a day sooner.

Why would I recommend that the Do-Gooder set aside money in retirement programs or annuities? Do-Gooders are generous by nature, and this, though a magnificent quality to have or find in a human being, can be a bit detrimental to a serious saving plan. For that reason, I would suggest that Tom put aside as much as he can afford in his retirement accounts. Since this money is not immediately accessible, it would stand a better chance of being left alone until he can use it. Otherwise he might be too tempted to find an honorable cause on which to spend it.

Your Brothers and Sisters in Harmonious Idealism

The usual suspects: the Buddha, Jesus Christ, and that Gandhi was a fine individual as well. These beautiful peaceniks and the writings they left behind make the earth go round with far greater admirability than money ever has, but unfortunately none of them was ever charged with finding a socially responsible mutual fund, and that kind of advice just isn't in their books.

Preparing for the Unknown

Life insurance, although certainly an unpleasant term to the ears of most Do-Gooders, should also be considered if one has dependents for whom he needs to provide financial support. Again, the emphasis here rests in his duty as a provider and not in the monetary projections of riches into future years. Seven or eight years' salary would be a reasonable amount of insurance to carry, using industry-acceptable estimates.

Don't expect a Do-Gooder to sit down, pen in hand, and logically arrive at the precise amount. It's just not gonna happen. Permanent insurance in the form of a universal life policy may be another avenue for a Do-Gooder to accumulate money toward retirement. If his family does not need the protection during later years, he may donate the proceeds to the charity of his choice. However, during his lifetime, he could access the money in the cash value of his policy to augment his retirement income.

Are You a Do-Gooder?

You may consider yourself a right-brain thinker who doesn't mind an occasional stroll down logical lane, but if you have had to wipe a tear or two from your eyes during a holiday season Folgers coffee commercial (I have), it might be interesting to find out just how much you mix heart and mind when it comes to money.

Here is some food for thought. Remember that this is by no means a formal assessment of your personality. Its purpose is merely to help you deal with any possible money myths you may be hauling around in your backpack. You may be keeping yourself virtuous and in the poorhouse simply because you associate money with corruption, perhaps at an unconscious level.

Circle your response for each of the following statements:

1. I feel guilty if I spend too much money on myself.

   I agree   I disagree

2. I believe money is the root of all evil.

   I agree   I disagree

3. I spend more on worthwhile causes than on myself.

    I agree   I disagree

4. I put others' financial needs ahead of my own.

    I agree   I disagree

5. Living modestly is the only way to stay in tune with important human values.

    I agree   I disagree

If you circled "I agree" to three or more questions, chances are you are a Do-Gooder.

You are wealthy in spirit, and money in *your* hands can only do good in this world. Set yourself up in a regular savings program so you don't have to spend much time monitoring your accounts and you can devote your energies to cultivating the quality of your life and the lives of those around you.

A *Final Thought for . . . the* Do-Gooder

You walk through life radiating good feelings toward those around you. You are understanding, you can see past appearances, and you enjoy helping others. When your day ends, you feel fulfilled and satisfied because you have been able to provide the warmth that will curb the pain of the afflicted, to comfort those deep in sorrow, to give advice to those who don't know how to solve their problems.

Your way of participating in the world sometimes forces you to renounce your own rights, leave aside things that you want to do, keep silent on points of view that—you assume—would hurt others. Begin by allowing yourself to recognize your aspirations so that you may discover your own needs. You also have needs, and it is time that you make room for them in your life.

Look at it this way: Fighting for what is yours is good for you. But it's also good for those who try to take it away from you. Don't be afraid to fight. Every confrontation provides a measure of growth for both parties. Do whatever you have to do and say whatever you have to say without hurting others, but say it firmly and with confidence. Both parties become stronger when you engage in constructive confrontation, expressing your feelings and your situation humbly, and listen carefully to each other's point of view. The peace achieved after the storm will be much more valuable and lasting than one maintained precariously just because you are afraid of breaking it.

Recognizing what you want and going after it (without feeling guilty or remorseful) will leave you even more prepared to make the world a better place to live. You are as deserving of help as those to whom you give support and comfort. Begin by helping yourself and let others help you. You need a great deal of energy to carry out your mission in the world. The best way to strengthen your efforts is by nurturing yourself with the energy radiated by those around you. To achieve this, dare to ask for help and accept it joyfully. If you do, you will generate synergy with your surroundings and develop the "one plus one is three" concept.

Give yourself the place you deserve. Value yourself at least as much as others value you. Accept the gratitude of those around you without blushing. Leave aside, at least for a brief moment every day, your humble self-image and feel the joy of being a person who is loved deservedly. This is not vanity. This is not arrogance. It's just pride in who you are and in the good you do. Enjoy it. The list of people who you have helped is longer and the well-being you have provided them grows stronger every day. Make sure that your name is also on that list.

3

THE
DILIGENT
INVESTIGATOR

*Once Upon a Time, There Lived a Diligent
Investigator.*

*If only God would give me some clear sign! Like
making a large deposit in my name at a Swiss bank.*
—Woody Allen

It was a spectacular late-summer afternoon. Bill was driving his eldest son, Jimmy, to the baseball field for the championship game, and both father and son were filled with electric anticipation. Bill marveled at his progeny. In his opinion, the boy had a great athletic career ahead of him, if he so chose. They arrived at the field, Jimmy jumped out to stretch, and Bill began to scour the neighborhood for a parking spot. A while later, having parked, he found himself confronted with several stands' worth of bleachers from which to choose a seat.

After a half hour of internal deliberation over where to sit, Bill found a pretty decent spot from which to view his son in action on the diamond below. It was not too far to the right and not too far to the left and just high enough to be able to take in the whole field. Bill calculated that the sun would be shifting—probably during the third inning, which would surely bring some shade to his section in the hot afternoon. Yep, thought Bill, this was probably the best place to sit. Well, actually, the *very* best place to sit was two down, a spot currently occupied by the rapidly reddening mother of a shortstop.

Bill squirmed in his seat. If only he could see the coach better! Two spots down and he'd have an eagle-eyed view of the signals Coach was sending to Jimmy on the mound. Maybe if he just asked Shortstop Mom over there. It was crucial that Bill be in a position to process the minute points of the game, in order to make the practice pitches with Jimmy at home more efficient. Bill continued to eye the seat with envy. He could no longer even consider enjoying the game in this infuriatingly inferior spot. Bill drew in his chin, scratched behind his ear a bit, and got ready to poke Shortstop Mom in the shoulder when suddenly he saw Jimmy in front of the dugout, waving his arms wildly in the air.

Father stared quizzically at son as Jimmy continued to thrash about, throwing his head back and forth demonically. What on earth was wrong with that child? Bill noticed the boy mouthing something, something directed at him. What? Bill made out Jimmy's soundless scream:

No, Dad! Do not do that, Dad. Please, Dad. Sit down, Dad!

Bill looked innocently at Jimmy and raised his shoulders, palms up.

What?

You know what! With that, Jimmy grabbed the elbow of a passing teammate and began jabbing at him mercilessly in the shoulder as illustration.

"Hey, dude, what's the deal?" Jimmy's teammate shimmied out of his grasp.

"Sorry, man, I'm trying to keep my father from harassing Matty's mom to give him her seat. He will not be satisfied until he's convinced her to move. Then when he actually has her seat, it still won't be perfect, and he'll spend the entire game chair-hopping, then complain that he couldn't watch the game because everyone had taken all the really good spots. That's his MO."

Bill pulled away from the woman and settled uneasily back into his bleacher seat. Okay, fine, Jimmy. Maybe it was better this way (but probably not!). Boy, now that he reevaluated, he could see that the woman's seat was a terrible spot and dismally located for capturing the game on film.

Not that Bill had a camera.

He felt a pang of guilt as he thought about it. He wished he had purchased the digital movie camera he had been considering for months. He could sure use it right now. But there were so many models and so many features, so many things to consider and decide among. He had nightmares of megapixels and zoom functions. Then the notion occurred to him that even though it wasn't in vogue anymore, perhaps an old-fashioned film camera that he was actually comfortable operating would suit his needs better than those delicate digital numbers.

After four trips to the camera shop, each exponentially more stressful than the last, after hours of questioning the weary saleswoman, Bill had become overwhelmed and decided to postpone buying anything until he had a chance to research the models on the Internet over the weekend. That was three weeks ago. This wasn't the first time Bill had felt guilty for not taking action in time. . . .

Why Our Diligent Investigator Holds It All Together

The Diligent Investigator has a great eye for detail and a deep sense of responsibility and love for his family, a powerful combination. Every project becomes a journey to be fully explored, and when a decision is made, it is usually a very good one. The Diligent Investigator usually has no trouble at all designing the perfect budget or taking full advantage of every possible tax deduction in his favor.

Ten years ago there was the lovely Tudor house his wife, Angela, had adored and that they never bought because he insisted on waiting until he could go over the comps in the area from another real estate agent. The house was snapped up, gone, and now worth twice what they would have paid. Not the first time—nor the last—that they had missed out on a good investment either.

After the house incident, Bill had consoled himself with the fact that he just didn't know enough about the house, it never felt *perfect* in that way that he knew a purchase was supposed to feel. No matter how much research he did, he felt he was missing the last vital bit of information that would warrant some action on his part. Angela called it "paralysis by analysis," but Bill was positive that it was better to have one's options open than to act blindly. After

47

How He Lets It All Fall Apart

The Diligent Investigator's gift for details is a great asset, but any strength, when taken to an extreme, becomes a weakness, and Bill is so afraid of executing his research and inadvertently missing something that he is rarely able to reach a decision in the end, a practice that could cost him and his family a lot of money and a lot of grief.

all, you couldn't just trust the real estate agent to know everything there was to know about each house, or even to be honest to prospective buyers. He needed to do his own homework.

Bill sighed and let his mind return to the game. Jimmy was up at bat, and he knocked a beauty back behind the fence. Home run. Bill was overcome with pride. As Jimmy trotted triumphantly on his last stretch from third base, Bill felt tears in his eyes and wished just this once that he had defied his own instincts.

Will the Real Bill Please Stand Up?

While Bill has a tendency to get lost in the details and forget the big picture, he is also known to prepare for emergencies with apocalyptic zeal. Y2K was Bill's big project, but after failing to choose between home-bunker companies, his family was left with an enormous hole in the backyard and no bunker to show for it. He refused to put in a pool.

Bill is not the type that is in danger of succumbing to investment schemes, but he is usually more susceptible to fear than greed. That said, the Diligent Investigator often has an eye for quality and will frequently purchase gourmet food, fine clothing, and luxury items he deems to have met his standards—*if* he has dutifully budgeted for it.

You will most likely find Bill lined up in front of the post office at midnight on April 15—he definitely does his own taxes. This money personality loves planning, planning, and then planning about what he's going to plan for later. What drives the Diligent Investigator? The desire to be right, to be perfect, and to remain in control.

How to Work On Your Strengths and Around Your Weaknesses

Okay, let's level with each other. If you are a Diligent Investigator, you will never admit this to anyone else, but down deep, what you'd really like to know is how to lighten up and not be so hard on yourself. Your uncanny ability to nitpick can quickly transform into an inability to make a decision, and that indecisiveness can result in a vicious circle of self-doubt and procrastination. But you could have your analytical process pay off rather than hold you back as long as you can set some limits for yourself.

The Now

When you, Diligent Investigator, begin the process of making a decision that has to do with money, you may start hearing "voices" inside your head: They come visit you before you sleep and find ways to guest star in your dreams. You believe they are on your side; they certainly *seem* to be on your side, providing you with many useful warnings and a plethora of what-ifs. What if interest rates go up? What if I need the money before I planned to use it? What if I find a better investment later on? Those incessant voices should be the first warning sign that an endless loop of in-decision lies ahead. It is time for intervention on your part.

The first counterattack begins with a reprogramming of the brain. For example, if you are pursuing the "best" house, the "perfect" camera, the "most comfortable" sofa, the "highest-paying" CD, etc., rethink your syntax. In-stead of finding "the absolute best," try to substitute the words "best" and "perfect" with the phrase "good enough."

You may wish to find a house that is "good enough" for you and your family to comfortably afford, a camera that is "good enough" for you to carry and still take "good enough" pictures, a sofa that is "good enough" for you and your wife to cozy up on with your dog and watch Monday Night Football, a CD that pays you "good enough" interest so you can stay ahead of inflation. By rephrasing your needs this way, you will be simplifying the whole process and you will feel a lot better about your final decision. When you see yourself beginning to obsess by looking for "the perfect one" of anything, remember that "good enough" is indeed good enough.

Also, try to replace the words "I ought," "I should," or "I must" with terms like "I want," "I wish," or "I would like." What you think you *should* do may make logical sense when looked at from a technical point of view—like perhaps getting the highest interest on your holiday savings account at the bank across town. But if what you'd really *like* to do is something else—say, have an account at a nearby bank where you know the tellers, even though it pays you one quarter of a percent less in interest each year, it's okay to opt for plan B. You don't always have to choose the best solution—just look for the one that makes you the happiest. Period. End of story. Let it go.

The Future

Here are a few tips for the Diligent Investigator.

If you usually run ten financial reports each month from every possible angle, it's time to simplify the process.

Choose the two that will give you a good picture of where you are financially, and eliminate the rest. You should commit to looking at how your investments are doing no more than once a month. Set a limit of time to ponder a financial project and stick to it. Give yourself credit for timeliness.

Don't overcomplicate potential projects by taking into consideration unnecessary details. For example, write a list of things to consider. Now divide your list into two lists, "must consider" and "might want to consider," making sure you have the same number of items under each heading. Get the first one done. Let go of the other one.

Give up the idea that you have to do everything on your own. Use a financial adviser as a sounding board. Think of him or her as a decorator, someone who, based on what you have established as important to you, will bring you some samples. Keep the samples to a manageable number. Let that person hit the pavement for you so you can spend your time bringing some balance into your life with activities that may involve your family and friends rather than crunching the numbers alone in your office.

It is time for you to explore new territories of possible gains by crossing the imaginary line between "savings" and "investments." A savings account represents a temporary parking space for your money—typically for two years or less. There are several places where you can make the most of your savings and still have the security of knowing that your money is guaranteed. CDs, money market funds, T-bills, and two-year notes are common tools used by savers who wish to earn a higher rate than they would receive in a regular savings account and still know that their money is safe.

There's a lot to be said for safety with your money. After all, the thought of losing money does not appeal even to the most aggressive investor. However, there is a very likely possibility that if you keep all your money in these types of accounts, you are "growing poorer safely," because they are not keeping up with the worst enemy of them all: inflation.

Let's say that you did your homework and you found a savings account all the way across this great nation of ours that pays you 4 percent. You deposited $1,000. Feeling pretty good about yourself, you relax in your favorite chair and casually glance at the headlines of the business section. "Inflation reaches 3%," you read. What does that mean to you and your savings account? Let's take out our trusty calculator to find out how much interest you would earn in one year on your recent deposit.

One thousand dollars multiplied times 0.04 (which is 4 percent) equals $40. If the interest rate in your savings account stays at 4 percent for the next twelve months, you will have earned $40 on your savings. Your money is safe, and you'll be ahead $40. Not bad. But unfortunately, that's not what you get to put in your pocket. If we have an inflation factor of 3 percent during the next twelve months, your $1,000 will lose 3 percent of its value. One thousand dollars times 0.03 equals $30. You will not see your bank account decrease by $30, but when you take that same $1,000 to the store, it will buy you $30 less than it did just one year ago due to the increase in the cost of the goods you are buying.

If you are making $40 in the bank, but your money is losing $30 in value, your net return for the next year would be $10, or 1 percent interest in bankers' terms. But the insult does not end there. If your savings account is not part of a pension plan such as an IRA, 401(k), 403(b), etc., you will receive a cute little statement at the end of the year from your bank reminding you that you must declare the interest amount in your tax return. Now comes the next whammy! Depending on where you are in the scale of taxes offered by the IRS, you will have to share part of your earnings with the government—even if you have not withdrawn the money from the bank! Your tax bite could range from $5 to $16.50 on that $40 interest.

If $10 was all you had left after inflation, you could actually be paying out of your pocket to make up for the taxes due, resulting in having less money at the end of the year than you did at the beginning. That is what I mean by "growing poorer safely." Inflation is nasty, nasty, nasty, and unless you are willing to consider investments that have traditionally kept their returns well ahead of inflation, you will be taking one step forward and two steps back with your money, any way you want to look at it.

My advice? Establish a "mad account." Give yourself permission to deposit 2, 3, even 5 percent of your take-home pay into an account that you will use to invest in a mutual fund or a stock. Consider it your bingo money and force yourself, if necessary, to do something other than keep it "safe" in the bank. Follow one system of investing, and be consistent in your criteria to buy and sell. If you learn to cut your losses short and ride your winners, you won't have to be right every time to come out

> *Remember, you can't steal second if you don't take your foot off first.*
> —Mike Todd

ahead. And the best part is that you can invest without the help of any adviser since you can open mutual funds and brokerage accounts with the help of your computer.

Are You a Diligent Investigator?

By now, you probably have a pretty good idea of whether you are or not, but just in case, here is a fun way to make it "official."

Circle your response for each of the following statements:

1. When it comes to vacations, I love to plan every detail and expense.

   I agree   I disagree

2. At the end of each month, I can tell you how much I will have left almost to the penny.

    I agree   I disagree

3. I would rather save than invest.

    I agree   I disagree

4. If I had a slogan, it would probably be "There is more than one way to skin a cat."

    I agree   I disagree

5. When I feel down in the dumps, spending money is not what I do to make myself feel better.

    I agree   I disagree

If you agreed with three or more of the statements above, you may be getting lost in the minutiae of your life. Stop calculating and start living. There comes a point where you may just have to hold your nose and jump! Remember, you don't have to know *everything* before doing *something*. You may exhibit your discomfort at first by continuing to investigate some details you may consider vital. This is normal. You may not get rid of your fear, but you can learn to act in spite of it. You are capable and consistent, and although you may not be able to control everything, you can handle anything that comes your way!

A Final Thought for . . .
the Diligent Investigator

Have this in mind: The best way to learn is through experience. Nothing else will instill confidence in you or enrich you nearly as much. Motivate yourself and act upon it, put into practice all that you have learned, incorporate your observations, and support them with facts.

Think of a baby, about a year old, who is learning to walk. The only way he can do it is through trial and error, by falling down and getting up repeatedly. Think of someone who did not learn how to swim as a child and wants to try later on in life. How do you think this person will succeed? By reading manuals and studying physical laws that explain the mechanism of flotation, or by practicing? Obviously the child will not learn how to walk along the edge of a mountain and the nonswimmer will not attempt to swim in the deepest part of the pool. The risks involved in each case should be considered. The same occurs with your daily decisions. Do not be afraid to make mistakes. Do not pretend to have everything under control. Since you are so good at analyzing even the smallest detail, don't forget this: Besides considering the risks at hand, don't neglect the risk you take in *not* making a decision.

There comes a time when there is no alternative but to decide to move forward. Decide to buy, speak, sell, invest, or whatever else you are considering. This is the moment when it is better to err while trying than to be paralyzed by the theoretical security of inaction. The security is theoretical because when one decides not to decide, in most cases, one ends up regretting it. The uncertainty and anguish that you feel when you must make a decision without having all the facts in hand should be replaced with the satisfaction of being able to decide based *only* on the necessary facts. You will enjoy the present and at the same time prevent future regrets.

Here's a tip—one hundred years ago, the Italian economist Wilfredo Pareto realized that in his own country, 80 percent of the wealth was controlled by 20 percent of the population. Years later, based on Pareto's research, Dr. Joseph Juran established what is known today as "Pareto's Law" or the "80/20 Law." This is how it works: 20 percent of the causes explain 80 percent of the consequences. For instance, a firm's customer service department receives one hundred complaints every month. It then determines which four causes for the complaints are the most common among twenty. Resolving these four issues would eliminate eighty of the hundred monthly claims received. By concentrating attention on the most important 20 percent, one maximizes the efficient use of time and effort. Try utilizing Pareto's Law at decision-making times. You will find that it can help you to become more efficient.

4

THE
DIONYSIAN

Once Upon a Time, There Lived a Dionysian.

"Why bother about winter?" said the Grasshopper.
—Aesop

It hadn't been just a party. It was the kind of blowout that made the Roman saturnalias and vomitoriums look like those pained, insufferable office birthday "celebrations." It was the kind of gala bash where the George Plimptons and the Pamela Andersons mingled like the fabled lions and lambs over elaborate ice sculptures and fondue fountains spewing globs of molten chocolate in a perpetual cascade. It was a sumptuous soiree the likes of which would never be seen again . . . that is, until Dean deigned to let his imagination and his receipt-signing hand run wild once more.

Dean turned the corner in his sleek new black Beamer, stifling a yawn as the tangerine-hued dawn drew up from the horizon, reminding him of the late (early?) hour, when he suddenly realized he still had one last errand to run before he could hide under the covers and sleep until the sun began to fall behind him. Groaning at this remembered task, Dean made a U-turn and headed back down the street.

"Daddy Warbucks" Dean had spent a bundle and a half on tonight's shindig, but he really got off on making people happy, on providing an atmosphere of good cheer and better booze. He was a manic giver of gifts that were so lavish, so over the top, that sometimes his friends dreaded receiving them, if only because it meant they would have to reciprocate to some comparable degree. Dean fancied himself a modern-day treasure hunter—like Indiana Jones with an Amex instead of a whip! When an ex-girlfriend had expressed admiration for an antique Amish buggy, it was gift-wrapped in her driveway at Christmastime. When she had joked, "Where's the pony?" Dean's face fell. Of course she would need a pony—how else to pull the buggy? He remained unconvinced when she attempted to explain she was kidding.

Dean hadn't wanted this evening to end. He had danced for hours to the three-piece band he had hired. He was particularly impressed with the roving magician. The performer had managed to keep the crowd engaged and thoroughly entertained, making money appear and disappear

Why Our Dionysian Keeps It All Together

The Dionysian is a master networker, a wonderful communicator, and an arbiter of ideas and innovations. If this personality type is out of work or luck, it is more than likely that he's accumulated enough goodwill (and Rolodex entries) to see him through the hard times.

from their pockets, handbags, even their ears! He longed for the magician to be with him when the bills arrived. He didn't know exactly how much all this was going to cost, but he was sure it wouldn't be cheap.

Well, it really wasn't his fault. This party had taken on a life of its own, and once he had started the process of planning, he didn't seem to be able to keep tabs on the charges. The ideas had flowed out of the party planner's lips as fast as the molten chocolate from the fountain. "It's probably fine," Dean thought. It was his mantra, really. "No cards were rejected. That's gotta be a good sign, yup. Everything will work out. It always does."

Dean turned in to an empty parking lot to complete his last errand of the evening. He trudged inside the garishly lit convenience store, purchased his biweekly lottery ticket from the unsmiling clerk, and prayed quickly but sincerely that *this* time it would make all his dreams come true.

How He Lets It All Fall Apart

The Dionysian is a notorious procrastinator, avoider, and responsibility shirker. If he does not rein in his spending, he faces massive debt and the loss of personal relationships that he holds dear.

Will the Real Dean Please Stand Up?

Dean has a good job, plenty of friends, a nice car, and a lot of debts. His taste for expensive clothes, good wine, and lavish parties has taken a toll on his finances. He has no savings accounts of any kind and no money set aside in his employer-sponsored 401(k) plan.

After paying his rent, car lease, utilities, and other monthly obligations, there is no money left over for anything else. In fact, Dean is beginning to use cash advances on newly acquired credit to make the minimum payments due on his cards. So far, he has managed to stay current, but recently he has begun to experience a new, rather unpleasant nagging sensation in the pit of his stomach. He has once or twice awoken in the middle of the night, a cold sweat on his brow—and the fear that he is caught in a downward spiral that could get him in a lot of trouble weighing heavily on his mind and heart.

Dean grew up in a one-stoplight kind of town. Intent on experiencing more than his family ever had, Dean announced his decision to move to New York at a relatively young age. His family had been so worried about their sweet Dean—fearful that someone would take advantage of his open arms and open wallet. But he had gone to the big city anyway, determined to prove to the folks back home that he would make it.

There were months when Dean's bills added up to more

than he made, and to make up the difference he frequently used one of the checks that arrived with one of the monthly credit card bills. It was so easy! Write the check, deposit it in his checking account, and, voilà! The balance in his account would immediately swell back into black. All was well again. . . .

But it wasn't. It doesn't take a psychiatrist and a couch to see that Dean feels loved when he gives. He has come to accept debt as a normal state, and he uses his plastic power to gain affection from others. He is always the one who picks up the bill at a restaurant and the one who pays the shared taxi's fare, sweet as an *occasional* gesture, but a symptom of potentially self-destructive behavior with short-lived benefits when taken to an extreme. In the end, Dean feels lonely and dissatisfied with his standard of living. Unconsciously, he uses spending and shopping as a way to stay removed from his need to be liked and his feelings of insecurity.

A Dionysian frequently:

- Is impulsive about buying decisions.
- Shops frequently in malls and large multipurpose stores, "open" to ideas for things to buy for others.
- Makes purchases that are not necessarily expensive, but are high in frequency.
- Has no budget.
- Uses credit cards and is likely to be in debt.
- Keeps minimal or no record of money spent.

- Feels that saving money is boring and impossible to do.
- Is usually outgoing and active, and has many friends.
- May use shopping catalogs and TV shopping channels when not able to go out and shop.
- Lives by the motto "You can't take it with you."
- Believes that, when in doubt, you should go with your gut, and his gut tells him to go ahead and spend.

How to Work On Your Strengths and Around Your Weaknesses

Fortunately, if you are a Dionysian, there are plenty of investment opportunities that will satisfy your desire for action and your zest for life. But first you need to learn to *control* your spending instincts. It may seem wildly counterintuitive at first, to save instead of spend, but anyone can do it with help.

CREDIT CARD 101

Eyes bigger than your bank account? Please consider the following exercise as a means to help you rein in your wild ways:

- Keep one credit card in your wallet. Place the rest in a home safe.

• Write down on a piece of paper the following questions, and wrap the sheet around your one credit card. Ready? Here they are:

> Where am I going to put this item?
> How will I use it?
> How often will I use it?
> How many hours will I have to work to pay for this item?
> What else could I do with this money?
> How would that help me?
> Can I live without buying this?

Next time you reach for your credit card to make a purchase, read the questions before handing over the card to the salesperson. If you still feel strongly about your purchase, go ahead. Otherwise, tell her you have changed your mind, put your card and your note back in your wallet, and walk out of the store.

The Now

Wait until you see the fun that awaits you, oh, my exuberant one, when you decide to make your money multiply without having to work so darn hard for it! If you are willing to take a time-out before you spend another penny that doesn't go to reducing your debt, feeding your face (and

I'm not talking restaurants or take-out food here), or keeping yourself warm and safe and at home, I think you will be rightfully revved up when you discover the stock market. Honey, it was *made for you.*

I may not know you personally, but if I had to describe you, I'd say you are a keen observer of details and trends, you are ready to take action quickly, and you are not paralyzed by the thought process. Am I on the right track? You can approach a problem from many angles and come up with a creative solution. You can work effectively in an unstructured environment because rules have a tendency to suffocate you. You love to engage in activities that have an immediate outcome and high impact.

If you find yourself smiling as you read these descriptions, then you are the perfect candidate for the mother of all investments: Welcome to the stock market. As an individual you are able to be part-owner of any company in the world that offers a little piece of itself for sale in the open market.

You don't have to be rich, you don't have to have a doctorate in finance, and you don't need to understand the fellows in the brightly colored smocks signing madly on the trading floor. You *do* need to commit some time and reserve some brainpower. You *do* need to make sure that you are not walking into anything with blinders on.

Why do people like you and me buy stocks? Because we hope to unload them onto somebody else in the not-too-distant future for a price higher than the one we paid. A stock may become available for purchase if a formerly private company decides to go public. If, say, a family-owned business wants to get extra money for expansion, to conduct research, or even to send the heir to an Ivy League school, they must raise capital. Yes, they could borrow money from the bank. But that means that the company would have to repay that loan with interest, which is not always the most appealing of options. They can also decide to cut that business into little pieces, like a puzzle. Each small part of that puzzle represents one share of stock. A company goes public when they offer these parts for sale on the stock market.

Google, the Internet search engine—and my most trusted ally while writing this book—went public in 2004, offering their precious bits of company at a starting price of $85 per share.

Each share of Google reached the price of $300 in less than one year from its IPO date (initial public offering, or "coming-out party"). Imagine, if you'd purchased ten shares of Google on that day, you would have paid $850 for them (plus the transaction fee that you must pay when buying and selling shares). Months later, you could have cashed them in for $3,000! Do I have your attention yet? Good!

In all fairness to you and to keep you far away from the padded walls and the white suit, I need to tell you that not every stock does as well as Google. We don't even know that Google's shares themselves will continue on their upward trend.

When the price of a stock changes, that new price represents how much per share you would receive if you sold it. Think of it as buying something "as is" in a garage sale with no guarantee that it is going to work once you get it home. But the risk involved in investing in the stock market can make the thrill of the hunt for the right stock that much more thrilling.

I don't know if you have noticed, but when women go to the restroom in a restaurant, other women in the group tend to join in. Perhaps this happens because mother nature sends an urge signal to the rest of the group, or maybe it's just the fact that we like to congregate somewhere away from our men for a moment of bonding. Whatever the reason, though, women are not the only ones who follow this pattern. Stocks tend to flock together too, and usually, when one stock in an industry goes up in value, other companies that belong to the same industry go up in value, creating a trend that feeds on itself until some event of consequence puts a stop to it.

It is common for shares of companies in a particular industry, such as medical stocks for example, to begin to increase in value at the same time. A successful investor will take advantage of this phenomenon by identifying what is in vogue at the moment in the world of investing.

Luckily, it is not necessary to be a stock detective, scouring the industry for the Googles or the Microsofts. Instead, we can buy the whole bunch in one fell swoop, counting on those companies in front to bring their weaker siblings along for the exciting ride up in price.

This type of investment is a relatively new breed in the fauna. It's called an exchange-traded fund—alias ETF. Don't let the name scare you; they are simply "baskets" of companies that, like some underwear, come in packs of more than one. Each dollar you invest in an ETF is equally divided among all the companies in the group. The corollary to the ETF is that once you are investing in this manner, you cannot pick and choose which stocks to keep. If you sell, everything goes. Exchange-traded funds have hilarious names such as Diamonds, Qubes, and Spiders, among others.

Qubes, for example, represent an ETF that has grouped the technology-focused stocks that make up the NASDAQ 100 Index, while Spiders hold the five hundred companies that make up the S&P 500.

How do you find the best ETF to buy? If you are like me, you prefer to look things up in your computer rather than thumbing through the newspaper or combing through endless journals and specialty magazines. A great shortcut is www.morningstar.com. This site offers you basic information about exchange-traded funds, what they are, and how to buy them. This site in particular possesses an invaluable screener page, and here you will see the different ETFs and how well they have done over the years.

If you have felt in the past that investing in mutual funds is as exciting as watching paint dry, but you do not yet trust yourself to select, purchase, and sell individual stocks on your own, ETFs may satisfy your innate need for speed while providing you with a reasonable amount of security, knowing that you have not staked it all on one company.

INVEST WITH YOUR FRIENDS

If you are a people person by nature, a marvelous and inexpensive way to get involved in the stock market is to form an investment club. An investment club is simply a group of friends—I've found that ten or so is an optimum number—who join together and pool their monies, smarts, and experience to invest collectively in the market.

Investment clubs are a blast—what's not to love? They are planning meetings disguised as parties, personal fundraisers masquerading as social hour—and best of all, you needn't contribute more than $10 to the common pot each month. Talk to friends you trust to join you in this venture; you might be surprised to find out that they too have been wondering how best to navigate the market on their terms. A great place to find out how it all works and how to keep track of your money in the club is www.bivio.com.

Investment clubs serve as a great social outlet, an enjoyable way to help you make money *instead* of spending it. You won't need to meet at the mall or a restaurant. Instead, each month, a different member of the group hosts the meeting in his or her home.

I have witnessed investment clubs do what countless financial advisers, myriad self-help books, and prolonged therapy could not—reform obsessive, thrill-seeking spenders and morph them into investment minimoguls. Discovering a lucrative investment is the ultimate shopping experience, and you get to share this joyful high with your friends and loved ones. Your meaningful relationships will deepen alongside—and not at the expense of—your pockets.

The Future

Once you begin to focus your energies on enjoying the process of smart investing, it's time to address the other end of financial success: how to control the money that goes out.

If I ask you how you are doing financially, you may think to answer in terms of how well you are able to meet your obligations on a monthly basis. But this shortsighted perspective of your money situation forces you to lose sight of the big picture. To really succeed financially, you need to open your mind to the consequences of *every* decision you make. For example, let's say that you are going to buy or lease a car. If you are using the "monthly mentality," you would probably figure out how much you could afford to pay each month and, armed with this knowledge, venture out to the showroom.

Upon entering the car dealership, the salesperson will approach you, and somewhere during your conversation, the subject of the monthly payment will rise to the surface. That is a very valuable piece of information to that dealer. By disclosing the amount that you are willing to accept as payment for that beauty on wheels, you have shown your cards prematurely.

I have seen two buyers drive their dream cars out of the same dealership with the same monthly payment. One of them got a fair deal for the car and the other got shafted. How could this happen? The first one concentrated on the *total cost of the car,* while the second person was simply satisfied to keep the monthly payments low.

By focusing primarily on the final cost of the car, after all interest and fees are taken into account, you are able to compare the actual value of your purchase. Make sure you do your research (the Internet makes this so easy that you should be ashamed if you do not take advantage of all the information at your fingertips) before stepping into that dealership so you know how much money the dealer paid for the car and what its fair market value is. That is defined as the average price actually paid for the same vehicle in your area. This way, you will know how much profit the dealer is cashing in, and you won't fall for his "I'm really losing money on this deal" routine. You can find that information on sites such as www.edmunds.com.

Once you have established the total price of the car, work on the payment terms. Don't forget to multiply the required monthly payment by the number of months it will take you to pay for the car. That amount, minus the cost of the car, represents the fees in interest or other charges that have been tacked on to your account. Many consumers also use the amount they can afford to pay each month to credit card companies to gauge how much of their available credit they can use. This is a very dangerous practice.

If you make only the minimum payment due on a credit card bill, it will take you years to pay off your debt. For example, you may be able to manage the $20 payment to pay for that $1,000 stereo, but it would take over twelve years to pay it off if you paid just the minimum due each month with a finance charge of 17 percent.

If you multiply $20 by 144 months (twelve years), the real cost of that stereo would be almost $3,000! How long would you need to work to pay for it? Is it worth it to you?

So here are some recommendations to manage your credit card debt:

- Have a meeting with all your credit cards by lining them up like little soldiers on your dining room table.
- Write down on a piece of paper how much you owe and what the interest rate is on each card, as well as the 800 number for each company.
- Go to www.bankrate.com and check out the section on credit with the latest offers from companies with low to zero interest rates. Make sure you read the

fine print. In many cases, if you are late or miss just one payment, all bets are off and the rate you will be charged may skyrocket.

- Call the company charging you the highest interest rate and tell them that you are aware of offers at zero percent or a very low-percentage charge and that if they don't lower the interest they are charging you, you will transfer your account. If the person on the other side of the phone tells you that he or she is not authorized to make that adjustment, ask to speak with a supervisor. You will be amazed at how willing they are to reduce your rate in order to keep your business. The bottom line is that it is more expensive for the credit card companies to get a new client than to take a small loss with you.
- Once you have called each account you have, rewrite your list using the new interest for each account.
- You may even consider transferring the balance of the account with the highest interest to the one with the lowest. This will not only make more of your payment go toward reducing your debt, but you will also simplify your finances by reducing the number of payments you will need to make each month.

Before you conduct this exercise, visit the place on the Web where you can request a free credit report from each of the three credit bureaus, Experian, TransUnion, and Equifax. You will find an easy way to submit your request by visiting www.annualcreditreport.com. You are entitled to one free credit report from each bureau every twelve months.

It is very important that you keep a keen eye on your credit report because it can contain serious errors that may affect you for years. If you find an error, immediately report it to the bureau *in writing* and give them approximately forty-five days to respond to your request to correct it.

You may also be given the choice to pay a small amount to receive, along with your credit report, your FICO score. This number represents, on a scale from approximately 300 to 900, how you rate in the eyes of the lenders. The higher your score, the more attractive you become to a potential lender and the better the terms of the loan. But borrowing is not the only area affected by this point system. Employers, insurance companies, and even landlords can request your scores and, based on the results, make a decision on whether to hire you, insure you, or house you. You may learn more about FICO scores and their effect on you by visiting www.myfico.com.

MAY I HAVE THE ENVELOPE, PLEASE

While you are working on your debt elimination plan, you may have to learn about the "envelope system" to avoid overspending. It is a bit extreme, but for the sensory-driven Dionysian, the tactile, visual nature of the envelope system will yank the idea of budgetary spending from the fanciful to the physical.

This is how it works:

Make a list of the name of each expense you have each month, starting with your mortgage or rent, food, transportation, insurance (medical, homeowner's, renter's, car), utilities, cell phone, entertainment, clothes, etc. Designate one envelope for each of these categories.

Every time you get paid, cash your check and place the allocated funds for each expense into its corresponding envelope. For example, if your monthly rent is $400 and you get paid twice a month, you would need to place $200 in the rent envelope each pay period. When you have put the allocated amount for each particular category in the envelope, that's it, the money is gone and you are not to spend any more money on that category.

You can adjust the amounts periodically. And make sure you have one envelope with your name on it. That money is to be used for savings in case you have an unforeseen expense. This method is an excellent one if you can't seem to account for where your money goes, not to mention the savings you will see on ATM fees. It also frees you from the ledger or spreadsheet. To make your envelope system run efficiently, you can request a change in the billing cycle from your creditors to coincide with your pay periods. Most of them will be happy to make the adjustment.

It is a myth that income levels are the main cause of financial problems for most Americans. Poor spending habits are the clandestine culprit. Financial security can be based on a very modest income, and saving money can be a lot easier than you think.

For example, if you find yourself spending $3 on a bagel and coffee every day, that amount would add up to $90 per month or $1,000 per year. By skipping that bagel and coffee (but not breakfast! Try eating at home) and paying down your credit cards to the tune of $70 or so more a month, you will be saving hundreds of dollars a year and contributing directly to the reduction and, soon, elimination of your debt.

Becoming aware of how much you spend doesn't mean you have to eliminate every indulgence, but I am sure that you will find some purchases you make almost unconsciously that you could have avoided without decreasing the quality of your life.

Are You a Reckless Dionysian?

Your money behavior will be guided by an internal automatic pilot unless you bring it into the light of consciousness. Ask yourself the following questions to find out if your desire to be loved and accepted by living beyond your means is taking precedence over your own need for financial security.

Circle your response for each of the following statements:

1. I always live within my income range.
   I agree   I disagree

2. Each pay period, I set aside at least 10 percent for savings.
   I agree   I disagree

3. I find it very difficult to buy expensive presents for my friends.
   I agree   I disagree

4. If I had a slogan, it would probably be "Always save for a rainy day."
   I agree   I disagree

5. I rarely make more than one trip a week to the grocery store.
   I agree   I disagree

If you disagreed with three or more of the previous statements, chances are you are making a connection between your self-worth and your money by sabotaging yourself. Stop!

In your quest for social acceptance, you may have lost your most valuable asset—you! Take a step back. Stop being constantly on output, and ask yourself what really makes you happy. What is your passion? Do your friends know about it? Are you surrounded by people who inspire you to pursue *your* dreams? Or are those around you too busy pursuing theirs to notice yours? Don't get lost in the shuffle. Carve out the place you deserve in this world, not for what you do for others, but simply because you exist. It's your birthright. You deserve to be loved and appreciated. Don't settle for less. Not now, not ever.

A *Final Thought for* . . . *the Dionysian*

And you—what do you need? For a moment, forget about other people's wishes. Forget about satisfying others. Look at yourself and ask, *Do I* really *know who I am?* Do you actually need to attract and charm other people? What would happen if you didn't? Have you asked yourself even once? This is my suggestion to you: For an instant, decelerate the speed of your life and allow yourself to think about what it is you want the most.

Do you really want to play the role that you have chosen for yourself? Do you like the character you have created? In life, we all play roles: We all conceive one or more characters. But a person cannot be summed up with a handy identifier. You are not a physician, lawyer, engineer, waiter, saleswoman, or journalist; you *work in* medicine, law, or whatever your professional field is. You are not bad-tempered, nice, resentful, humorless, or distracted. At any moment in your life—like many other people—you may decide to change the kind of work you do. And at any time you may change the way you face the world.

To be and to practice, to be a person and to be temporarily in a certain disposition or to have a passing feeling—these are two very different things. Your *real* essence, your inner being, *that* is what you are. You may occasionally be—perhaps too frequently—in a bad mood. But you *are not* a bad-tempered person. If you were, you would not have any opportunity at all to change. But you can change your attitude, your mood, or the activity you are involved in whenever you decide to.

Don't try to pass as the character you have created. Do not establish it permanently as if it were you. You are just as valuable as all those whom you try to flatter. You love to play. You enjoy having that slightly rebellious and quite entertaining image that you show to the world. Why not step out of character and play for a while? Stop trying to please others and instead notice what's happening. Maybe at first you'll feel uneasy, as if trying on a new costume. It's normal that you might feel uncomfortable at the beginning, until you get used to it.

Inevitably, a change of attitude creates changes in your surroundings. And that change creates a resistance. Therefore, chances are that those around you will feel as uncomfortable as you do with the new role they will have to play if you don't act as you used to. When you don't ask for the check in the restaurant, when you don't jump to take the initiative, another person will have to do it instead of you.

If you can't afford to buy someone his or her dream gift, buy what you honestly believe this person will like. In selecting it, do it carefully and with love, and have in mind that it does not need to be perfect. If it's only good, it will do. Many times, an object considered perfect by someone is, according to another, a nuisance. That's why a good gift might be also good for both the giver and the receiver. Furthermore, do not hesitate to confess to that person that you would have loved to buy for her or him that special item that you know he or she longs for. Say also that you feel that what you chose is something special for her or him and that you can afford it. Sincerity is one of the most appreciated virtues among friends, isn't it? You will see that if you are able to prove what you are and what you can do, people's responses will be as authentic as your own messages to them.

Try to experience this change of attitude. You might get a joyful surprise in realizing that it's not so bad to feel flattered, that it is possible to connect with your desire and your true possibilities, and that you can be faithful to your new discovery. It's never too late to try.

5

THE DEPENDABLE HOARDER

Once Upon a Time, There Lived a Dependable Hoarder.

"I am having an out-of-money experience."
—Unknown

George had worked long and hard for every penny he'd ever possessed, for as long as he could remember. As a teenager, he would rise at dawn on weekends and trudge the half-mile to the stately, old-money neighborhood where he worked odd jobs for a loyal clientele of wealthy homeowners.

And it wasn't as if he used his earnings to buy comic books or take girls out on dates. No sir. The money George brought in every week was used to pay for school clothes for him and his sisters. After all, as his father always said, perhaps not originally but with conviction to spare, "Son, money doesn't grow on trees." George's father had hours' worth of money proverbs, saving methodologies, and careworn, homespun financial advice. George Sr.'s financial philosophies were all variations on what he saw as the one true fact of money reality: Keep it safely hidden away, even from yourself, and you will be assured peace of mind.

Now, with a family of his own, George was determined to continue the honorable tradition of frugality that he had learned from his parents. But it wasn't easy. Especially in this day and age! Especially today, actually. His normally quite reasonable wife was literally cornering him in his own kitchen.

"George," Sylvia said, one hand on her hip, and the other pointing a wooden spoon at his pockets. "George, I'm asking you very, very nicely. Please give me the checkbook." George closed his eyes and shook his head solemnly.

"Why not, George?" But if she didn't understand by now, how could he possibly explain it to her? How could she not see that their daughter absolutely, unequivocally did not need $200 for cheerleading outfits? Gah! Why had they even let her get this far? Cheerleading was dangerous anyway; she could fall off one of those ridiculous pyramids and crack open her skull. No no no. He couldn't even bring himself to discuss it. The absurdity was so obvious.

"George, I rarely say a word when it comes to the family finances. When you make popcorn at home and hide it in a shopping bag before heading out to the movies for our monthly treat, I applaud it. I never laugh when you drive twenty miles out of the way to fill up your tank at the station with the lowest gas prices in town. I have never raised objections to our silent consensus that there is never enough and we will always do without today, if necessary, in order to have enough for tomorrow."

Now she was being reasonable! George had always known that, no matter what the little guy did, the Man was going to get him in the end. The Man had a hundred different incarnations, from the government to greedy corporations, but a small fry like George would never have a shot against him. Even though money and the rising cost of raising a family was a common subject around the dinner table, how much money they had or how much money they would need in the future did not enter into any of their discussions.

"George, do not let the fact that I have let you get away with hiding the truth about our financial situation fool you into believing that I do not care. Remember the financial planner?"

"Yes, I remember. I went, didn't I?" George attempted to dodge the spoon, but Sylvia wagged it in his face, recalling the truth of the incident. A few years back and at her insistence, they had met with a financial planner. "Yes!" Sylvia had thought. "This will be the perfect opportunity for me to find out how much money we really have!"

Unfortunately, George never intended to answer the planner's questions in anything other than frustratingly vague terms: "Sort of," "Not quite," and "I only wish!" were the most concise of his answers. When the planner left, Sylvia was no closer to knowing their true net worth than she had been before. In the end, the planner was not able to offer any concrete financial alternatives to the couple. And even though George assured his wife that he would think about what the adviser had said, he never called him back. George had explained it away simply by stating that he didn't trust this "Joe person" who was probably "broker" than they were. So much for the financial planner. . . .

Only George knew where their money was—there, safely tucked away, just in case they needed it in the future.

And only he could look out for himself and for his family's financial security. Besides his numerous savings accounts, George kept some money in a safe deposit box in the bank, where he wouldn't have to pay taxes on his loot, not to mention his super-secret stash under the third row of tiles in the kitchen pantry. . . . Shhhhh! George couldn't help smiling to himself every time he thought how clever he was!

How Our Dependable Hoarder Keeps It All Together

No debt, no extravagant expenses, and an austere, if not downright monklike, outlook on spending keeps the Dependable Hoarder in the black most of the time. A lifetime of devotion and dedication to the art of saving will hopefully allow the Dependable Hoarder to be open to alternative forms of financial safeguarding.

This is a most interesting personality. Their incarnations can range from those who hide behind the excuse of a very busy lifestyle, too occupied with other matters to do anything about finances, to someone who down deep feels that money is synonymous with evil, to someone with a tremendous fear of scarcity, which really translates into the fear of losing control.

How He Lets It All Fall Apart

In one word: fear.

The Dependable Hoarder is terrified to death about the future and about the present, and is a true contingency planner. Unfortunately, the methodology with which a Dependable Hoarder goes about squirreling away his funding is most often tragically misinformed. In the end he may be left with much less than originally anticipated, plus the gut-wrenching sensation of having failed in all that meticulous stockpiling.

George may crave invulnerability, but he has a difficult time finding it. In the name of security, George has vowed to himself that, if he has enough money tucked away, he will always be safe and no person and no catastrophe can ever harm him. Money becomes a shield that guards against all danger. What is in the bank is referred to as "sacred money," not to be touched or even *thought about*. To George, it was a one-way street. Once in the account, it ceased to exist. Unfortunately, his secret stashes are giving him a false sense of security, and when it comes time to take a serious look at the state of his finances, he may come to realize his pots of gold are quite a bit smaller than when he first hid them.

George, like many clients who have come to me over the years looking for that kind of financial security, needs only to discover that his bottomless money pit will never be full until he realizes that *it already is*—if only he allowed himself to "feel" safe.

Prototype of a Dependable Hoarder

A Dependable Hoarder is usually reacting to past disappointments. The silent mantra of a Dependable Hoarder is: "Even if nobody comes to my rescue, I will make sure that my money will be there for me, and I won't have to rely on other people who may disappoint me."

Yes, your money personality is really the result of your own deeply personal interpretation of the experiences you have encountered along the way—even if they no longer serve a purpose.

> *The more [money] a man has, the more he wants. Instead of its filling a vacuum, it makes one.*
> —*Benjamin Franklin*

If you were raised in a home where money was used as a symbol of corruption and the people in possession of it were looked down upon, chances are that you are going to feel guilty if you spend—or even make—a lot of money. If you heard a parent or someone with authority in your household frequently say things like, "That's not for people like us," "They are filthy rich," and "Money doesn't buy happiness," you can't possibly feel very good about yourself if you make or spend your money.

If you are broke, you will be afraid that you will never make it, and if you manage to have some money, your fear will usually manifest itself by preventing you from even appearing to have it—a guard against others envying or criticizing you. No matter what happens, you end up feeling poor, inferior, unlucky, and vulnerable.

Are you a Dependable Hoarder? Take a look at the following characteristics of this personality type and find out for yourself:

You are Dependable Hoarder if you feel that:

- All your money is going to go away if you're not careful with it.
- It's not safe or prudent to spend money now because you might have to do without in the future.
- Forces outside yourself are primarily responsible for your financial status.
- Savings accounts are by far the most preferred strategy for preserving money.
- When saving, it is more important to concentrate on the return *of* your principal than the return *on* your principal.
- When it comes to money, it is better to be safe than sorry.

- Comparison with others who are doing worse than you are makes you feel better about yourself.
- It is better not to know than to be disappointed.
- It is better to avoid failure than to achieve success.
- Since people can't be relied upon, it's better not to count on them.
- It is honorable to live below your means.
- You are not a good receiver—not necessarily due to pride, but to feelings of mistrust and vulnerability.

How to Work On Your Strengths and Around Your Weaknesses

At the expense of getting a little mushy, I need to gently remind you that, even though your main concern as a Dependable Hoarder may be your fear of running out of money, the first step toward achieving the happiness and satisfaction that money may bring to your life is to make sure that you don't run out of life itself.

You may be very good at accounting, but put your abacus aside for a moment and answer this question for me: Have you taken an inventory of your life lately? What I mean by that is, have you asked yourself about the quality of your life, the time you are currently spending with your family and loved ones? Is it in balance with the amount of time you spend worrying about money?

Time is money, they say. Well, yes and no. Money and

time are intrinsically related: You can *save* both of them and you can *spend* both of them, but you can't *make* both of them. You may be able to make some more money once it's gone, but once time is gone, it's pretty much impossible to manufacture more. So, how you spend your time today—and tomorrow—really should have more value to you than how you spend your money, don't you think?

The true value of money, then, rests with the quality of the time it can buy you. If you really want to feel the power of security that your money can bring you, ask yourself the following question: How much money do you need to have coming in every month for you to comfortably spend your time in a way that would truly make you feel happy and closer to those around you?

Instead of focusing on what can go wrong in the future, concentrate on what you wish for your future, and then begin to take steps to make sure that happens. As you develop the goals that are meaningful to you and your family, remember that you are going to have to battle, more than once, the vows you have unconsciously made to yourself along the way.

You may be planning how much money you need to set aside in a special vacation account for a family trip to the Caribbean, and your inner voice may be creeping in and softly whispering in your ear that "it's an unnecessary and extravagant trip that you don't really *need.*" Believe it or not, this inner voice may be more powerful than what you consciously believe you are pursuing. You must be vigilant at all times—acknowledge its presence and dismiss it, forbidding it to sabotage your new, healthier path.

The Now

Try to locate the source of your craving to hoard your money. Maybe saving for a vacation was something your parents could not afford to do, given their circumstances. But that doesn't mean that the same applies to you here and now. You can rewrite your script once you realize that your less fortunate past is interfering with a promising future. So sit down with a paper and pencil—and don't forget your family—and follow these steps:

- Make a wish list for each member of your family and for the family as a whole.
- Give it a timeline of when you would like to accomplish each item.
- Next, ask yourselves how much money you will need to have in order to achieve each goal.
- Now, and I know this one is probably going to hurt because you are on virgin territory here, take a look at all your accounts—yes, even the one underneath the tiles—and assign some money to each worthy cause. You may be pleasantly surprised to see that you have already reached some of your goals without even realizing it. Go for it! Enjoy them!

For those of you who have not reached your goals yet, establish a realistic savings plan. Remember that hoarding means oversaving without a legitimate reason. By giving a *purpose* to each of your accounts, you will feel in control of your destiny as you get closer to its realization. You will allow yourself to enjoy the feeling of accomplishment as you reach each goal.

I don't expect you to turn into a daredevil with your money. But I do want you to familiarize yourself with some of the accounts that are available and that will offer you a better return than you have been receiving in a regular savings account or—sorry to rub it in again—under the tiles in the pantry, and that will still appeal to your conservative and protective instincts when it comes to your money.

Dependable Hoarders Throughout the Ages

History is littered with eccentric characters who danced to the beat of George's meager tune. And it didn't have anything to do with the amount of money in their bank accounts.

Let's start with a woman by the name of Hetty Green (1834–1916)—the richest woman in the world at the time and yet someone who conducted her business sitting on the floor of the Seaboard National Bank in New York, amid trunks and suitcases full of her papers, simply because she didn't want to pay rent for an office.

Hetty was so frugal with her money that when her son, Ned, broke his leg as a child, she tried to treat him at home to save money and ended up having to have his leg amputated because of neglect. Ned had to wear a prosthesis made out of cork for the rest of his life. Even though her net worth was estimated at around $100 to $200 million dollars, Hetty wore the same black dress and undergarments until they literally fell apart.

Or how about J. Paul Getty, who became the richest man in the world in 1957, and who had a payphone installed in each room of his seventy-two-room mansion in England?

And then there is Uncle Scrooge McDuck, the famous Disney character who, in spite of his vast fortune, is still hanging on to his very first dime.

KEEPING IT SAFE AND SMART

Let's pretend that you want to keep $1,000 or more in a safe place and that you are willing to refrain from touching the money for a period of at least five years. If we have 2 percent inflation a year, your $1,000 will buy you only $980 worth of groceries by the end of the first twelve months since the cost of living has increased by that 2 percent figure. The nerve! Leave it there and watch it lose another 2 percent of its value the following year. It's as if your money takes two steps back for every year that it remains in your secret place.

At this rate, at the end of the five years, your $1,000 will be worth only $903.92. That means that you have *lost* almost 10 percent of your purchasing power. Your money may have been safe from Ali Baba and the forty thieves, but it definitely was not secure from the greedy little termite we call inflation. With this little bit of information, you can begin to see that, in order for you to stay ahead of the inevitable deterioration of the value of your dollar, you must be able to make a profit on your money, a sum that at least equals inflation.

The Future

So, would it be of any interest to you if I told you that there is a type of account that not only guarantees you that you won't lose any of the funds you deposit, but will also guarantee you that it will fix whatever damage inflation causes by making up the difference? This type of account is called TIPS—which is short for Treasury Inflation-Protected Securities.

TIPS are offered by the U.S. Treasury, the branch of the United States government that handles and distributes the revenue necessary to run all governmental offices. Part of this revenue—besides the money that the government gets from taxes—comes from loans we can make to the government. These loans are called Treasuries. Treasuries are considered to be the safest of all possible investments, since they are backed by the U.S. government itself. TIPS, then, are Treasuries that adjust the balance of your account up or down, according to the rate of inflation, to make sure that when you withdraw your money, every dollar you deposited is worth the same amount it was worth the day you made your initial deposit.

I love the philosophy behind TIPS, and I wish we could apply it to more than just money in an account. Wouldn't it be great if we could be guaranteed that our wedding dress will still fit on our twenty-fifth anniversary the same way it did the day we got married? Oh well. For now, TIPS will have to do. But that's not all, because besides offering you this guarantee, TIPS will pay you interest on your money twice a year, and you won't have to pay local or state income taxes on your gains.

"What's the catch?" you, the most suspicious of all money personalities, ask. You *must* be willing to leave your money alone for the period established at the beginning of your agreement, which could be five, ten, or twenty years. You can find out more about TIPS by visiting the official government site at http://www.publicdebt.treas.gov.

YOU CAN ALSO CHOOSE DOOR NUMBER TWO

If guarantees appeal to you, but you wish to have the possibility to earn a higher return than savings accounts or TIPS, you might be interested in an annuity. An annuity is an account that you open, not with a bank or even the government, but with an insurance company. There is no blood test and no medical exam required! An annuity is simply a type of account where you deposit your money in exchange for an interest payment. There are two types of annuities: fixed and variable.

We will cover only fixed annuities here, since a variable annuity uses your money to invest in mutual funds that could possibly lose value over time, and I don't want you to turn the page without hearing me out.

In a *fixed annuity* you are making a long-term commitment, since these accounts are meant to be used for retirement income. You must plan to use your money when you are 59½ years of age or older, but not a day before. If you are willing to leave your money alone until then, or if you already are past that age, then a fixed annuity may offer you the opportunity to earn a higher return than you would receive in a savings account (some fixed annuities called *index annuities* pay you a rate based on the increases in the value of the stock market), and still give you the assurance that your money will earn a guaranteed rate of return, usually around 3 percent per year.

Another advantage of annuities is that you don't have to pay income tax on the gains you receive in your account until you withdraw the money. That means that your account will grow much faster than it would if you had it in the bank, where you would have to declare your yearly profits at the end of each year and pay taxes on them, even if you didn't withdraw them. As you can see, my dear Dependable Hoarder, there are places where you can put your money to work for you and still satisfy your need for security.

Your homework is simple—give each account a definite purpose and explore these two alternatives, which will take you beyond your natural comfort zone and will make you expand your knowledge of money management. You will see that when you add purpose to your craving to save, you will begin to feel more in control of your money and your life.

Are You a Dependable Hoarder?

Just in case you are still in denial, here is a list of five questions I want you to answer for yourself to see if fear is the driving force behind your financial decisions.

Circle your response for each of the following statements:

1. When I was growing up, I got everything I asked for.

   I agree   I disagree

2. My parents were comfortable with money and felt rich, even when they didn't have much.

   I agree   I disagree

3. As a child, I received a generous allowance that allowed me to get what I wanted.

   I agree   I disagree

4. My parents' money was often spent on pleasurable family activities.

   I agree   I disagree

5. I never heard my parents say, "We can't afford it."

   I agree   I disagree

If you answered "I disagree" to three or more questions, you may need to make an appointment with your little voice inside and reassure it that you are perfectly capable of caring for yourself and your family without having to resort to hoarding your money out of fear.

Security is mostly a superstition. It does not exist in nature, nor do the children of men as a whole experience it. Avoiding danger is no safer in the long run than outright exposure. Life is either a daring adventure or nothing.
                                                        —Helen Keller

Take the skeleton out of your financial closet. It's not about collecting the largest amount of money. The feeling of abundance comes from:

- Knowing that you really do have as much as you need.
- Knowing that, even *if* something catastrophic happened, God forbid, you could rely on your own smarts and abilities to satisfy your own basic necessities.

A Final Thought for . . .
the Dependable Hoarder

Being fearful is not necessarily bad. Fear is one of the wisest, most evolutionarily ingrained mechanisms of defense we have. At times, it is necessary and even indispensable to be afraid.

Fear is not the issue: How one reacts when facing it determines its usefulness. When fear paralyzes and hinders your activities, it is no longer something positive—it becomes your master and you its slave, denying you the experience of new and exciting challenges.

Our fears exist to entice us to do something to help us grow. Our most precious dreams are waiting to be realized, and the door to them is hidden behind our fears. When fear seizes you, don't cross your arms—much less run in the opposite direction. Get ready, keep your eyes open, and move forward to defeat it. The mere fact that you have decided to overcome and defeat your fears changes the situation. Although you still have fears, you are a different person. When you identify which actions have to be taken to finally meet your fears and are adequately prepared, you begin to realize that nothing is as terrible as it can appear.

Living your life in full, instead of merely surviving, requires taking risks. I am not talking about learning to parachute if you are terrified of heights. I'm referring to calculated risks: risking a cold by allowing your child to become drenched during a warm summer rain, or enjoying without guilt an enormous chocolate ice cream sundae despite the risks of an upset stomach or a few extra pounds.

Ask yourself, "What's the worst that could happen?" For every fear that limits you, ask yourself what's the worst that can happen if you go ahead anyway, and you will pleasantly discover that the worst that could happen is not worth considering.

> *Happiness means being happy with less rather than being unhappy because you wish to have more.*
> *—Unknown*

Dare to challenge your fears. Dare to confront them. You are well-equipped to know when you are ready and when you still need to prepare yourself a little more. Once you have overcome your fears, you will find—besides the enormous internal satisfaction that this brings—that you're decidedly moving toward achieving your most beloved dreams.

The
Relationships

6

MONEY
AND
YOUR KIDS

Danielle was the first to arrive. She tumbled out screaming bloody murder, the kind of wailer who becomes the stuff of legend around a maternity ward. Amy, on the other hand, glided into the world with the grace of a prima ballerina.

It was a highly auspicious beginning.

After a few months of having the two little ones home, their mother became secretly convinced there had been a hospital mix-up. How else to explain her babies' polar-opposite dispositions, habits, schedules, even facial expressions? She wondered whether or not her other real baby was like Amy—sweet, pacific Amy, content to spend hours staring at the mobile above her crib, who slept with an enviable Zen-like tranquility and accommodatingly ate when presented with food.

But perhaps the kid was more like Danielle—hilarious, demanding Danielle, who required constant human attention and had an almost spooky need for eye contact. Her well-developed lungs were ready to fire at any time of day or night if her labor-intensive needs for entertainment were not met.

The twins' physical resemblance was overwhelming evidentiary support that counteracted their mother's theory, but still she marveled at the extraordinary differences between the two, who seemed, at first glance, so much alike. The differences continued to manifest themselves, no less certainly than on their first day of nursery school.

Most parents have vivid memories of this momentous day, and this family was no exception. The girls were decked out with lunch boxes in hand, in pretty, new first-day-of-school frocks and shiny patent leather shoes. Danielle wore a yellow ribbon in her hair and Amy a purple one, something that their mother thought would help the teacher identify them. Turned out she really needn't have bothered. Two minutes after their arrival, there was no mistaking the two girls.

Danielle took to school like a fish to water and made friends right away. Once inside the classroom, her big brown eyes scanned it speedily. Danielle then let go of her mother's hand and strode up to the crafts table, where she immediately started a conversation with two other girls who were making globs of something out of their globs of Play-Doh.

Amy glanced shyly around the playroom as she clung to her mother's legs. She was not in the least interested in what was going on in that place full of noise and strangers. In the end, her mother had to tear herself from Amy's grasp with the help of the kind teacher who reassured them both that everything would be all right. It took Amy a good two weeks to stop crying when her mother dropped her off in the mornings.

After the adjustment period, Amy seemed to welcome the structure of her school day. Her teacher included periods of physical activity, followed by quiet-time projects, such as art, story listening, and naptime. Amy's favorite activity was circle time. Although she didn't share any of her experiences with the rest of the children, she seemed to enjoy the stories that were told, and she sat in her place quietly and contentedly until it was time to move on to the next task.

Her sister, Danielle, looked forward to school every day too. She didn't seem to stop talking about her scholastic adventures from the moment she got up until the moment she went to bed. She was a bubbly child who willingly shared her toys, and this made her very popular among the other children. Danielle's favorite activity was also circle time. She loved having everyone's undivided attention as she went into detailed accounts of her half-true, half-imaginary stories. Danielle couldn't understand why her teacher didn't think it was appropriate for her to share with the class the combination of her family's safe.

By the time the girls were in high school, little had changed. Danielle was a champion debater and in the prom and homecoming courts all four years. Amy belonged to the chess club, the math team, and was the treasurer of her class council.

Will the Real Sisters Please Stand Up?

How do you think Danielle's natural tendencies toward socialization will translate into the way she will manage her money as an adult? How do you help an outgoing, spontaneous, and carefree child learn to become self-sufficient without crushing her zest for life? Could she turn into a Diva or a Dionysian?

What about Amy? Do you see her handling her money the same way as her sister? I doubt it very much. Amy's cautious approach to life may very well translate into a cautious approach to money. Would you say that she would prefer to keep her money close to the vest? Do you think she would be a saver or a spender? A Dependable Hoarder or a Diligent Investigator?

So how do you share a healthy attitude about money while you allow for the differences in your children's temperaments? And here is the kicker—how do you find the balance between your own preferred style and theirs? The first step is understanding that your children are already giving you clues to their individual preferences and that these preferences will affect the way they relate to money and how they will interpret *your* money message.

Whether we like it or not, we are all born with our personalities, hardwired into our DNA. Sure, environment plays a role in how these inborn traits are played out in each of us, but we bring factory-installed tendencies that influence the way we view, process, and relate to the outside world and that affect the way we approach and try to solve the problems that come our way.

So if you are under the (unfortunately mistaken) impression that children are born with an absolutely clean slate, and we as parents get to fill in our preferences for their personalities, perhaps you haven't encountered, as I have, two bewildered, bespectacled parents, fluent in crossword puzzles and philately, staring uncomprehendingly at their offspring who, despite his physical resemblance, seems to speak only hockey and comic book.

As parents, you may delight in the fantasy that our children are pretty much the same as we are—a chip off the old block, an extension of our own personalities who will naturally follow in our footsteps. The reality of it is that your child is who he or she is, and no amount of fretting is going to change that fact. If you remove the fangs from a lion, you might end up with a toothless lion, but never a house cat. When you try to forcibly change your children into what they are not, the end result can be an emotional scar rather than a healthy transformation.

> *Who are these kids and why are they calling me Mom?*
> *—Unknown*

The goal for you as a parent with an interest in teaching good financial habits is to look at your child maybe as someone you do not completely understand, but whom you can come to appreciate without crushing his initiative along the way. The role that parents play when it comes to shaping these attitudes can be immense, and yet few families actually talk seriously about money with their children.

"Not me!" you exclaim. "I'm always telling my kids how hard it is to make money, how expensive the cost of living is, and how important it is to save and not waste it." Great! Let me ask you this: Do you show your children how *your* family money is spent, saved, or invested? Studies show that those who have managed to save and invest a significant portion of their annual income can recall that they had frequent conversations among their family about these subjects. In fact, as a family member, you have more influence on how your child will handle money in the future than his or her own spouse.

How soon should you start discussing money, saving, and investing with your children? The following experiment will tell you if they are ready to learn: Hold a $5 bill in one hand and a $20 bill in the other. Ask your child to choose one. If he chooses the $20 bill, it's time to start. Do two out of three if you don't believe your eyes. Your child will know the difference between the two bills around the age of six. This might seem a tad young to get started, but as with conversations about smoking and drugs and the dangers of strangers, you can tailor a conversation about money to any age, and the younger they get a sense of what you are trying to communicate, the better chance you have of getting the good stuff to stick.

Your Child Is Ready, Now What?

Whether you are filling in the gaps for your children about money matters, or starting with a very young child who is just beginning to assert himself in ways that affect your home economics—in other words, he or she frequently utilizes the term "I need" for things like video games, Bratz dolls, and various other "necessities" of life (I call these assertions "eyebrow archers")—it is a good idea to have a specific goal for what you need to address. Here is a guide that will help you.

Teach children that there are three things you can do with money:

You can acquire it

There is no denying that you need to make money at some point in your life in order to become a financially independent person. You can talk with your children about how your family makes money—and get ready to be asked how much money you make. I usually told my children that we made enough money to take care of our needs and give to those who were less fortunate than we were. This is usually a sufficient answer for younger children. For older kids—those who can grasp more complex financial ideas, such as the cost of living in your town—you may wish to give them a truthful approximation.

How your children can "make" money while living at

home is a decision that only you can make. Some parents use money as a reward for good grades or good behavior. Sometimes an allowance is viewed as a salary that is given out as payment for services rendered—taking out the trash, doing dishes, or teaching Dad to program the DVR. When my children were growing up, my husband and I tried to teach them the difference between "making money" and "creating a money-making opportunity."

We stressed the latter as the more dynamic and interesting way of going about the business of obtaining cash. To that end, my children never got allowances as salary. Our theory was that chores were there to be shared among family members. We all eat, we all help, sometimes more, sometimes less, but we do it because we love one another and respect the efforts of each member. As far as money was concerned, our family unit had one pocket, and out of it came what each of us needed and sometimes what he or she wanted.

When my children asked me to buy something I felt they did not need, I would look them square in the eye and ask: "Can you give me five ways you could possibly create the money you need to get what you want?" They did walk away from me rolling their eyes on more than one occasion, but eventually I got some pretty good suggestions regarding what they were willing to either compromise on or contribute to generate the money they wanted. And best of all, they could then purchase that video game or gooey chocolate bar without a lecture or interference. That was my first contribution to fostering the concept of financial independence in their minds. This notion can be absolutely exhilarating to kids: a parental yoke they can, with Mom and Dad's blessing no less, cast off in favor of their own determination and hard work. How does your child acquire money?

A Diva child may feel that he is entitled to an allowance, regardless of his personal contribution to the household or his parents' financial situation. If Mom and Dad do not agree, this type is also the first entrepreneur on the block as well—get ready to choke down a lot of lemonade.

A Do-Gooder child will end up accumulating money without ever having set out to collect it. Birthday cash and the occasional loaded handshake from Grandpa will combine to give this type of kid a hefty little nest egg. It's right about this time that she'll ask you how exactly to address an envelope to poor children in third-world countries.

A Diligent Investigator child will want to know now about any trust funds you have set up for him, and when exactly he can have access to them. He'll want to work for his money, and will very possibly have a kind of squeegee-man mentality about it: "Well, I *already* alphabetized your CDs, Mom. Don't you think that's worth at least a few bucks?"

A Dionysian child will probably just ask for money a lot, having already spent and/or lost whatever he began the day with. Check his shirt for telltale signs of ice cream man visitations, or his room for any exotic new "pets" if you just can't figure out what he's doing with it.

A Dependable Hoarder child's income will be a collection of loose change found in couches, in addition to other creative ways of acquiring extra cash. Apocalyptic fear of not having enough, or worse, her parents running out, will compel this child to bravely seek it out wherever she can.

You can use it

Once the kiddos get some money, and if you are not too strict about what they are allowed to do with it, their first forays into money ownership will provide you not only with more clues to their personalities, but most likely a good chuckle or two as well.

Let children help pick out a charity that the family can all agree upon. When you are out shopping with your children, explain your purchasing method. How do you balance price and quality concerns? Why do you shop where you shop? Using the parameters your family requires to stay within budget, let them pick out items they feel fit the mold.

A Diva child spends at the rate it comes in—and sometimes gets a little ahead of himself by spending his money *before* it gets to his hands. Watch out for this child becoming monstrously in debt to a Diligent Investigator sibling.

A Do-Gooder child is usually frugal and careful with his money. A Do-Gooder child loves nothing better than holiday and birthday time—the better to spend his dough on gifts for those he loves. Encourage him to save a little as well, instead of going overboard on wrapping paper and ribbons.

A Diligent Investigator child may feel she is a minimogul at an early age. This child wants calculators and will insist she can figure out Quicken, just give her a chance. She'll spend her money on tools she feels will maximize her money—a lot like the young Ben Stiller character in *The Royal Tenenbaums*.

A Dionysian child relishes his ability to satisfy his whims to buy. This is the kid in the front seat of the shopping cart, eagerly reaching and pointing and totally unshy about stating his preferences. Encourage this kind of child to really understand why he values what he values.

A Dependable Hoarder child is the money-saver par excellence; his piggy bank is his best friend. He holds on to as much money as he can, often hiding it from his family and from himself. This kind of child is likely to stash fivers around his room, forget about them, and find them five or fifteen years later stashed in a book or under the mattress.

You can manage it

This is actually the process you use to decide how much, in what manner, and when you will spend or save your money. Your individual money-management process dictates everything from how you pay for your newspaper in the morning to how you handle your retirement investments. The differences in personal style can range from the micromanaging to the chaotic and out of control.

Let your children witness you balancing a checkbook or creating a monthly household budget, and offer them the opportunity to learn how they can pay for what they need and also reserve a portion of what they make for future wants and needs. It's also a great excuse to show them how you figure out 10 percent.

Even very young children can learn to "wipe out" the number on the right to calculate 10 percent of a number. I would ask my children to write a two-digit number that they knew—the end result would undoubtedly be one of the TV channels they enjoyed most. Next, I told them how I was going to wipe out the last number (right and left may be a hard concept for younger children). I proceeded to dramatically obliterate the last number until they only saw the remaining numeral. That numeral was 10 percent of the original number. So if we had twenty, I would wipe out the zero at the end; the remaining numeral two was my 10 percent.

From that point on, every time we went to a restaurant, they helped me figure out 10 percent of the total bill to calculate a tip—from figuring out 10 percent it was a very easy jump to the 15 or 20 percent we would actually leave. Your children can deposit 10 percent of the money they get in a savings account, piggy bank, or jar. This is probably the best habit you can teach your child about money. It allows them to be disciplined with the least amount of pain, and at the same time, it frees them from feeling guilty if they spend the rest. You may wish to have them save 10 percent and give 10 percent to charity. The concept is the same.

How Far Is Your Apple from Your Tree?

Once you know your children's tendencies and your own, it becomes much easier to establish the most effective method of communicating with them about money. You can also help them understand how their natural profiles can help or hinder them in all aspects of their lives. By learning to work around their weaknesses and maximize their strengths, they will end up seeking a balance and being much happier and accepting of themselves and others.

The Diva child
Children who are Divas in the making will usually value more expensive items. This poses a real need to bud-

get to avoid blowing savings on an impulse buy. Get ready to tackle the status labels because what his friends own or wear will have a definite impact on him.

This child may also be more susceptible to advertising than the other types. Try to avoid letting him get his hands or eyes on too much of it. Utilize the DVR function of your cable provider (if you have it) to fast-forward through ads when you're watching TV with your kids. DVDs without commercials are another way to block out those irksome ads. Encourage this type of child to be open-minded and make up his own mind about his preferences—before the outside world gets a chance to influence him.

The Do-Gooder child

You may show him how to save money by getting a pet at the local animal shelter rather than the pet shop at the mall. The key here is to show that you can get what you want and do some good at the same time. He does not need to choose between these two important concepts.

Encourage him to read about companies that have a conscience while they do good business. You can search the Web for socially conscious companies. Encourage him to learn to choose the most profitable companies within the "good guys" and research them to consider buying their stock.

The Diligent Investigator child

Precise budgets and projections will just flow out of this child. You can purchase simple future-value calculators at most office supply stores and online. These nifty little gadgets will help him do future projections of small amounts of money at different rates of return, calculate how much he needs to set aside each month to reach a particular financial goal, and many other findings that will satisfy his need to look at something from every angle.

It is important to help him decide the parameters that are "good enough" for him to make a decision. You may have had the experience of taking your child to the toy store with some money and very little time to spend it, and then walking out in frustration because he couldn't make up his mind as to what to buy. You are better off deciding exactly what he wants before you leave your home.

The Dionysian child

If your child is a Dionysian, don't expect him to be able to stick to a budget without some help from you. Since money just seems to run through his fingers, you are better off keeping a running balance for him if he's saving for a goal. Keep the time frame short. Remember that there are too many temptations for this fun-loving type to spend his money and deviate from his original plans.

If you give an allowance to a Dionysian, do it weekly rather than monthly to help him budget his money. You may have to help your child stick to his budget by using the envelope system, where he assigns one envelope for each spending or savings category. This method will help him visualize the division of his money and stick to his plan with less anxiety.

The Dependable Hoarder child

If you have a Dependable Hoarder at home, you already know that he loves to be surrounded by his possessions. Your child will probably enjoy collecting coins in a see-through container, where he can admire his progress. Encourage your child to begin investing early on. Discussions about inflation are very beneficial for a Dependable Hoarder to understand. Help him realize that there is more risk in doing nothing with his money than in making an occasional mistake in judgment.

If your Dependable Hoarder buys a stock, it would be a good idea to have him actually receive the stock certificate. Being able to "look" at his company every day will satisfy his need for security. You can actually buy just one share of stock by going to www.oneshare.com. When you order a single share of stock from this site, you can choose to have it framed and have your message engraved on a brass plate. This makes a great gift for a newborn or someone who came to the United States from another country. It is a great symbol of actually owning a "piece of America." This stock would not be viewed as an investment (although it does have the value of any other share of the company), but as a great reminder that we live in the best country in the world, where we can actually be part-owners of the companies that we support.

Investing is akin to driving while looking in the rear-view mirror because there is no guarantee of a return, but by showing your Dependable Hoarder child the best and the worst scenarios in the stock market, and what the average return has been over the past seventy-five years compared to other methods of saving, you can help him expand his instinctive conservative boundaries.

Now then, you may wonder why I have been stressing adjusting the conversations about money with your kids to their personality types. After all, *you* are the grown-up. You pay the mortgage, put clothes on their backs and food on their table. Shouldn't your children do things the way you do? Why should you be the one to change your ways to adjust to the little critters? Does this all mean that you have to turn into a "yes" parent? Is this whole personality thing just a bunch of touchy-feely philosophy? Not at all.

You will be able to improve your ability to manage your money by "borrowing" from one or more of the other personalities that complement your instincts. If you make the effort to understand your own motives behind your money behaviors, you will be more likely to have a positive influence on the behavior that your children will adopt as adults. Remember, there is no right or wrong way to do it. What you are trying to achieve is a balance. If you display any of the extremes in acquiring, spending, saving, or managing your money around your children, it will have an impact on how they will handle their own finances.

You don't have to agree with your children, but you are older and wiser than they are, and it is in your best interest to learn what makes them tick so you can get what you want—I mean, what's best for them—out of them, especially when it comes to teaching them about money. The payoff of learning what your child's personality is will ripple out to other areas as well.

A middle school in Minneapolis conducted an experiment with a team of four sixth-grade teachers who volunteered to learn about personality types. They agreed to introduce the students to their individual personality types. Utilizing the information, the teachers adjusted their lesson plans and teaching styles to incorporate the variances.

After one semester, the grades and attendance rates for the students assigned to the pilot team were better than for the other sixth-grade classes. Why? Because the experiment had helped the teachers build solid relationships with their students, and when you build a relationship, you have added a vital ingredient to the learning process. By understanding your own personality traits and how you interrelate with your children and *their* individual traits, you will have an easier time defining yourself as a parent and as an individual, with an added bonus of improving how you yourself manage and enjoy your money. The most amazing thing about the Minneapolis experiment was that behavioral problems declined sharply as well—a definite bonus to any parent.

I have two sons, Tony and Jonathan. Tony is a combination Dionysian/Do-Gooder. He used to give his toys away when he was little when he saw that his friend didn't have something he had. I remember that when Tony was around two years old, we used to sing a song about a mommy duck with a dozen ducklings. The song lamented the fact that the ducklings had no shoes. Oh my! He came crying to me when he realized the meaning of the words and begged me to take him to the store to buy shoes for the little ducklings!

At twenty-two, nothing has changed. I don't know how many of his friends I ended up feeding on a regular basis in college because Tony felt sorry for them when they could afford only peanut butter and jelly until the next paycheck. To Tony, money has always meant options, fun, and freedom. My perennial parental wish for Tony is that his bank account be as big as his heart. To that end, I convinced him that he is a good candidate for direct deposit, and taught him how to channel his outgoing and risk-taking personality into solid investments. He now invests in the stock market, though he has more trouble selling a stock (he was always a very loyal child!) than buying it.

> *Children seldom misquote you. In fact, they usually repeat word for word what you shouldn't have said.*
> *—Unknown*

Jonathan, on the other hand, at nine years of age displayed the characteristics of a combination Diligent Investigator/Dependable Hoarder. When he was a little boy, he wanted to keep all the toys and clothes that no longer fit him *for his children,* and it was very difficult for us to convince him that they should go to others who needed them more than he did. To Jonathan, money has always symbolized security. He also invests in the stock market, but as soon as his stock begins to go up in price, he gets the urge to sell it because he is afraid that it will go down and he'll lose his profits. For Jonathan, we've made it a point to stress the ebb-and-flow nature of the stock market and to educate him about the history of the stocks he does own, in the hope he'll relax and relinquish his urge to overreact.

It's a Small but Different World

Our children have many more options than you and I had growing up. Think about it: it was difficult enough for us to choose among the thirty-one flavors of ice cream at the store, yet today there are over forty kinds of coffee beans at Whole Foods Market, over two hundred channels on DIRECTV, and if you have gone to a Starbucks lately, you may have noticed that placing your order can sound more like a dissertation in Italian than a simple request for coffee.

Our adolescents are taking more time to search their souls and choose their life paths, and it is very difficult for them to think long-term about most

> *A father is a guy who has snapshots in his wallet where his money used to be.*
> *—Unknown*

things, including careers and financial security. They are not just looking for a job to pay their bills; they want a meaningful career that will give them a sense of purpose and importance. They are also expected to live well into their eighties, and for that they will need to make sure that their money does not run out before their bodies do.

A Final Thought On . . .
Money and Your Kids

Khalil Gibran said, "Your children are not your children. They are the sons and daughters of Life's longing for itself . . ." You are an instrument, a tool to help your children develop, but they are distinct individuals, and they are different from you. They are different human beings free from their mothers' wombs, even if that connection was indispensable to them for a few years after birth, and even if they decided to stay with you for some more years. The sooner you understand this situation, the better it is for you.

Surround them with love, but be careful not to choke them. Care for them as they need to be cared for, but never prevent them from learning how to take care of themselves. Do not confuse love with permissiveness. If you are excessively strict with them, in time your inflexibility may trigger the end of the relationship.

Quality is more important than quantity in your relationships with your children. Nowadays, it is not uncommon to find that children are raised by their grandparents, by nannies, or in child care centers. That is why it is essential that the time you spend with your children is entirely dedicated to them. In those moments, come out from behind the newspaper you are reading, show your face, and notice their presence. If you are anxious to check your e-mail, both of you will be frustrated by your child's inability to captivate your attention; you'll end up feeling defeated and frustrated, and you will grant whatever they wish just to stop them from nagging. However, before deciding what to do—pay attention to your child, or take care of the "important" task—ask yourself which of the two is really the important one.

When they grow—and problems will also grow—you will regret how many hours you wasted during their childhood. Ask them what they think about you, ask them about their likes and dislikes. Do not be afraid of their answers. In any case, don't be afraid to modify your behavior.

If you are too strict, before answering "no" to their next request, ask yourself, "Why not?" Picture yourself in a few years talking to your kids and being in a position of having to answer when they ask, "Why did you never let me do what I wanted to do?" There is still time to avoid that question.

If, on the contrary, you are a parent who finds it difficult to set boundaries, the question you will probably have to answer at some point in their adolescence or adulthood might be, "Why did you allow me to do it?" In the end, your children might consider your permissiveness a sign that you didn't care. Don't ever allow that to happen.

Once and for all, don't lecture. Talk to your children on a level they can understand, listening attentively and giving them the same respect you demand for yourself. After all, that's what they are—human beings deserving of the same rights their parents have, and frequently better equipped and smarter about themselves than their parents. That's what they have always been, even before being born, even if oftentimes we parents take too long to realize it.

Don't try to be their best friend. Their friends are their friends. They are not expected to be their parents. Your children expect care, respect, love, and guidance on how to become an independent person from you. When you understand and accept your children, their growth will become the impulse for your own growth.

7

MONEY
AND
YOUR FRIENDS

L et's just split the check three ways, okay?" said Charlie, grinning as usual. He grabbed the check just as the waiter set it down on the table. Now, there's nothing out of the ordinary with this statement as you picture three friends out on a weeknight enjoying a meal together after a long day. But this blasé, assuming posture of Charlie's was beginning to get on Frank's nerves. He instinctively turned to see the look on Patrick's face when he heard Charlie's request. He was hoping for at least some recognition of the absurdity of this proposal, but instead Patrick displayed no reaction. Frank sighed.

Silently, he and Patrick took their wallets from their back pockets, counted their money, and handed it over to Charlie, who was already tucking his credit card into the black leather pouch on the table. "It figures," Frank fumed to himself. "Charlie has just gotten a cash advance from his credit card without having to pay for it." Frank vowed to himself that this would be their last meal together.

"It's not that I'm cheap," Frank rationalized to himself on his way out of the restaurant, trying to justify his anger toward Charlie and his resentment of the evening's events. And he was right. Frank was not a miser. But Charlie, a gregarious and otherwise extraordinarily likeable character, pulled the same trick on them every time they went out to dinner together. Charlie had ordered a steak and an expensive bottle of pinot noir while Patrick and Frank settled for hamburgers and fries. And he thought it was acceptable to pay only a third of the bill? Not only that, Charlie *knew* Frank didn't drink.

The routine was getting old, and Frank wasn't going to take it anymore. Patrick, on the other hand, hadn't seemed disturbed in the least by the little restaurant scene. He was always willing to pay any price to avoid a confrontation, and this evening was no exception. But Frank had had just about enough. Who did Charlie think he was? What precious gift was he endowed with that negated his obligation to treat his friends fairly?

Frank didn't say a word as they walked out to the parking lot. He was furious with himself for falling into his friend's manipulative trap again, and worse, for not having the guts to say anything about it. Frank climbed into his car, slammed the door shut, and sped off without so much as a goodbye.

The remaining two men, startled by the eruption of Frank's engine and squeal of his tires, turned to each other in surprise. Charlie opened his mouth as if he wanted to say something, but he stopped as Patrick took a step toward him, held his arm, and said quietly, "You know that Frank's moody, Charlie. Just let it go."

Will the Real Friends Please Stand Up?

Each man had brought to the restaurant something besides a healthy appetite. Whether you are a Diva, a Do-Gooder, a Diligent Investigator, a Dionysian, or a Dependable Hoarder, your money personality goes with you wherever you go and plays a major role in all your interpersonal relationships. The truth is, this conflict had very little to do with the real feelings Frank had toward Charlie. He liked Charlie. *Everyone* liked Charlie. A typical Dionysian, Charlie was accustomed to stretching his finances as far as his plastic would allow . . . and beyond! This was not the first time that his lack of focus and discipline with money had affected his interaction with his friends. In fact, Charlie had an unusual relationship with most people.

Although not particularly handsome, Charlie, with his happy-go-lucky personality, dazzling wit, and impeccable taste in clothes, music, and books, was usually to be found at the top of party guest lists. He was a real lady-killer and made a great wingman. But his unrestrained spending was as salient and memorable a characteristic as his signature moves on the dance floor. His money habits became an intrinsic part of who he was and how he was perceived by the people around him.

He had few qualms about relying on his friends to bail him out of a financial jam. Someone always seemed to come to his rescue whenever Charlie got anywhere near a crash. His subtle distress signals created a vacuum that someone would rush to fill. No one stayed angry with him for very long. His bubbly personality left no room for hidden agendas. What you saw was what you got—and what you got usually cost you money. If you went out with Charlie, you would pay. End of story.

And most people did not mind chipping in for this jovial member of the clan, but no one could tell whether or not it was a sustainable condition. His friends referred to him as the Dependent. He was an expensive form of entertainment, and nobody wanted to be the first to admit that indeed, instead of helping Charlie, they were helping him perpetuate his weaknesses around money. It became easy for his friends to lord things over him, to remind him, pointedly or subtly, about his debt to them. It became easy to feel superior. Hmm, who was using whom?

Patrick, on the other hand, was a Do-Gooder. He figured that since Charlie obviously meant no harm, there was little good to be had in indicting him right there at the table (although he could sense Frank's indignant glare even as he did his best to ignore it). They had had a really nice dinner, before the whole payment fiasco. In retrospect, Patrick wished that he had just thrown down for the whole meal himself; he could have prevented the ill that Frank so clearly wished upon Charlie.

But Frank was not interested in Charlie's intentions.

He was furious at Charlie for his callousness and total disregard for fairness. Most of all, he was angry with himself for tripping on the same stone *again*. Frank was a Diligent Investigator who examined each careful move from every angle before taking action. How could he not have seen it coming?

Charlie's spontaneity was a mystery to Frank. How someone could buy a condominium without going inside even once was beyond his comprehension. And yet, that's exactly what Charlie had done. It had taken Frank three years to decide where he wanted to live and another two to find the perfect house for himself and his family. Frank had done his own research, delving into the catacombs of city records to explore any history of seismic movements in the ground or faulty levels in the water table of the area. He pored over city council meeting agendas to determine if there were plans to expand schools, move trees, or add roads, which would impact the current traffic flow. He knew what the crime statistics were, not only by city but also by city block, and he took the time to visit the areas that interested him at different times of day and night to verify noise, views, and travel time to and from work.

> *If a man does not keep pace with his companions, perhaps it is because he hears a different drummer. Let him step to the music which he hears, however measured or far away.*
> —Henry David Thoreau

"I got what I deserved," Frank snarled to himself. He had let his guard down, and that was something he was going to make sure never happened again.

A Man Is Not an Island

Three people, three money personalities, three points of view. Up till now, we've been focusing on understanding what makes us tick as individuals.

But, I mean, let's face it. I know that sometimes solitude can be bliss, but what is success without friends to love, enjoy, and celebrate with? Our money personalities profoundly affect how we connect with those around us. Social gatherings provide a background on which we display ourselves and our temperaments. When it comes to money, though, what you see is definitely not what you get.

Remember the Diva from chapter 1? She may choose to believe that people see her elegant ensembles as wholly appealing. But the unfortunate reality is that every time she buys something expensive to feel better, she's really adding one more brick to the wall that she's built around herself. Unbeknownst to her, her appearance—the expensive jewelry and designer clothes that are *supposed* to project an image of success and self-assurance—actually ends up intimidating those around her, the ones whom she so desperately seeks to wow.

She gives the impression that she has it all together, but people refrain from getting too close because they interpret her almost regal elegance as aloofness, and people tend to feel uncomfortable in her presence. She doesn't invite her coworkers or casual friends to her apartment. They assume it is because she has more glamorous friends, a social calendar that does not leave room for them, and—more pointedly—that she's a snob. What they don't realize, however, is that the reason she doesn't ask anyone to hang out is not because she thinks they are beneath her socially, but because she *doesn't have any furniture.*

You got it. The apparently calculating Diva would rather *wear* her money than spend it on her living space, where she might actually allow herself to get comfortable with herself or others. Her salary may pay for her counterproductive public image, but her private surroundings are the true reflection of how she really feels about herself—lonely, scared, unappreciated, and overworked—whether she is aware of it or not.

> *Money is the false guardian of our self-esteem.*
> —Kathleen Gurney

How do others perceive the Dependable Hoarder? Frequently as the guy who gives the lame Secret Santa gift and never chips in for office birthday parties.

People tend to see bleeding-heart Do-Gooders as silly, hapless humans who may never get a hold of themselves financially. The less scrupulous among friends and family alike will see a Do-Gooder as nothing more than a mark. While our Do-Gooder believes he is projecting peace and "Kumbaya"-style harmony onto those around him, by continually picking up the tab, giving ill-advised loans, and not caring if people view him as weak, he unfortunately allows himself to become so.

A Dionysian like our Charlie will try desperately to make people love him, but more often than not he will end up alienating his friends, and no one can be expected to support a grown man's entertainment budget forever.

Our Diligent Investigator, with his charts and his constant advice and his near-condescending attitudes about money, can also turn people off to his well-meaning words of wisdom.

Personal Loans 101

If you are financially independent, bereft of debt, and have a tendency to pay your bills on time, chances are that, sooner or later, you are going to be asked to lend money to a friend or family member. What should you do? It all depends on what kind of a lender you are. Here is a quiz that will help you figure out if you should open up for business:

Circle your response for each of the following statements:

1. Charging interest on a loan to a friend is acceptable.

    I agree   I disagree

2. If a coworker borrowed $5 for cab fare two weeks ago and hasn't mentioned it since, you would ask him for the money back.

    I agree   I disagree

3. After several instances of lending money to a friend until payday, you would offer to help her draw up a budget so she could learn to manage her money better.

I agree   I disagree

4. If your best friend asked you for a loan and you did not feel you would get your money back, you would be up-front about it and decline the request.

I agree   I disagree

5. If you had to borrow money from a friend, you would insist on writing a formal IOU with the terms of the loan.

I agree   I disagree

If you agreed with three or more statements, you can skip this section of the book. You don't seem to naively mix family, friends, and money. For the rest of you who didn't get that score, I offer the following suggestions on how to handle yourself in this type of spectacularly difficult situation.

Plan A is a canned speech you can have at the ready so you are not taken off-guard by the request. If someone you know asks to borrow money from you, repeat after me: "I love you too much to do that." That's it. Say the words, change the subject, and hope it never comes up again.

Plan A is unfortunately far from foolproof. Sometimes

you find yourself trying to deflect a tenacious would-be debtor, or you just can't bring yourself to brush him off. If you can't afford to just gift the money to your pal, or you really want to go ahead and loan him or her the cash, activate plan B—which at this point is the only chance you have to avoid a potentially disastrous situation in the future.

Handshakes and hugs may feel good, but they don't substitute for solid, written agreements if you are lending or borrowing money. Relationships can be destroyed and families broken due to misunderstandings about loan terms. According to statistics, a personal loan has a default rate fourteen times higher than the 1 percent of unpaid loans from banks. If you make a personal loan under vague conditions, you have a very good chance of losing not only your relationship but your cash too.

Before borrowing money from a friend, decide which you need more.
—Addison H. Hallock

This is a bit of friendly advice that really almost transcends financial personality types. No matter who you are, or whom you would loan to or borrow money from, there is a right and a wrong way to go about this delicate task.

Let's imagine the following scenario. Your cousin Vinny (a real Dionysian) has asked you to give him a short-term loan so he can expand his inventory in order to prepare for the higher sales he is sure to get during the holidays. Vinny promises to pay you back as soon as he gets the money from the big orders next month. You agree. You shake on it. You write a check. So far, so good.

Holidays come and go, and Cousin Vinny has not made one payment. The plot thickens.

There's a family gathering, and both you and Vinny are expected to attend. You are willing to refrain from mentioning the loan to your cousin out of respect to him and all those gathered. Vinny, however, feels so excruciatingly guilty about not having paid you back that he avoids you like the plague. This only infuriates you. The nerve! You feel betrayed. You gave this good-for-nothing the money, and he has the audacity to be rude to you. You should have yada, yada, yada . . . You feel your blood pressure steadily rising.

Can you see how quickly things can get out of control?

There is a way you can avoid this situation. Thus, plan B.

You say: "I'm happy to be able to help you by lending you the money you need, Vinny. That money is not doing very much for me right now, and I would rather see it go where it can benefit both of us. I'd like to set the loan up in a way that won't interfere with the loving relationship we have."

Tell Vinny that over ten million people in the United States have a private loan with a relative or friend and that there are companies that specialize in handling them. There are advantages to Vinny in formalizing the loan through the proper channels. As part of the process, a bank account is established to receive the payments, and the bank reports to the credit bureaus every time a payment is received. This will help him establish a good credit history as he pays the loan back. If the loan is properly set up, Vinny will also be able to write off the interest (should you decide to charge it) on his tax return.

Google "interpersonal loans" to find a number of companies that offer this service. Visit one of them and follow the on-screen instructions. You will also find free booklets to guide you through the process for immediate download. Either go over the Web site with your cousin or ask him to visit it at his leisure and call you when he's ready to proceed.

That's it. Put your arm around Vinny's shoulders, go have a drink together, and wait for him to call you back. He now has the information he needs to consider before borrowing money from you, he knows exactly what is expected—and you won't have to be the heavy.

Business Buddies

Ah, your heartwarming childhood memories! You may fondly recall your first lemonade stand. There you were, posing professionally by the table, feeling like a mini-maven as each car in your neighborhood stopped to buy the contents of your Dixie cups. You were simply irresistible—a true salesperson in the making.

Your best friend, Garret, was the administrative assistant and bean counter. His job was to make sure that enough cups were neatly arranged on the table so your customers wouldn't have to wait too long to be served. Garret's other tasks included dispensing exact change and lemonade making.

What a great way to spend a Saturday afternoon . . . that is, until your friend turned bossy on you and demanded that you be the one to refill the lemonade pitcher every time. So much for friendship and partnerships.

How to Pair Up Successfully

Say you are ready to take the world by the tail by turning into the Bill Gates of the dog-grooming business. You and your college buddy have been talking about it for months. The Traveling Sponge, as you've decided to call it. He has the van, the hose, and, heck, he even has three dogs of his own. And you? Well, you can sell snow to an Eskimo. You have the gift of the gab. Everything you need seems to be in place. You are ready to begin . . . right?

Wait! Not yet. Two heads are not always better than one. Before you take on your first furry client, let's consider a few things. Just because you can be the best of friends on the weekends doesn't mean that you and your friend will be great partners during the week. The acid test of a good partnership is whether you are really better off together than you would be flying solo. I would feel a lot better about your new venture if you and your friend could answer honestly and specifically the following questions:

- Do you consider each other's contributions as *crucial* to the success of the business? Why?
- What specific skill will each partner bring to the mix?
- Can you describe your business's mission in twenty-five words or less?
- What type of business structure will you use?
- Who will own the business? Ownership should be a direct reflection of the contribution of each partner, whether monetary or otherwise.
- How will you distribute the profits? How would you handle a loss?
- How will you pay for expenses? How much money will each of you contribute to the business?
- What will the role of each partner be? What happens if that role changes over time? Will that affect ownership?
- Who will call the shots? In other words, who will be the "tiebreaker" if there is a disagreement?

What if . . .

- One of you wants out? How will you assess the value of the business, and when and how will the departing person receive what is due?
- One partner marries? Divorces?
- One partner dies? I know, a horrible thought, but one you must take into consideration.

- Will you hire employees? When would you consider doing it? Who will do the hiring and firing?
- How does each of you communicate?
- Do you both have the philosophy of trust and transparency, or is one of you a "trust but verify" kind of guy?
- Are you both either pessimists or optimists? Do you see that glass half empty or half full?
- Do you have the same work ethic?

And here is the trickiest one of all:

Do you know your money personality and your partner's and how it may affect your business venture? Hint: If your friend is a Dionysian who chose to buy on eBay a three-legged stool where Elvis allegedly once parked his tush rather than pay his rent, are you willing to risk the substantial investment in time, money, and effort with a partner who may not be financially mature enough to truly devote all his resources to the goal of a successful business? Can you really afford to be the sole person in charge of damage control for yourself and your business, should the adventure fail? If, on the other hand, your partner is a Diligent Investigator, the ability of your business to grow may be hindered by his tendency to procrastinate decisions. Will this kind of hand-wringing make you want to tear your hair out on a daily basis?

If you and your friend still want to go into business together, may I suggest that you assign a trial period before you draw up any documents? How about doing a project together for the next three months? You can choose to divide net profits (after expenses) equally during this trial run. Go on and give it a try before you commit to formalizing the arrangement. If at the end of the period you evaluate the results and still feel that this is the best thing that could have happened to each of you, you have my blessing to pursue your dreams. Make sure you have a written agreement. You will find all the information you need to draw up your business plan and begin your new venture on the right foot by visiting the official site of the Small Business Administration at www.sba.gov. Good luck!

Sweating the Small Stuff

Your relationships with friends work best when you know yourself well. It takes hard work and a lot of courage to admit your hopes and to pursue your own dreams. It can take even more courage to recognize that the people around you are not necessarily those who foster an atmosphere of encouragement and goodwill. Once you are aware of your own personality and why you react the way you do under stress, you will begin to be more sensitive to the clues that your friends and coworkers constantly give you as to how they deal with money, success, fear, trust, and even friendship.

Listen carefully to what they say and how they say it.

Whether in business or pleasure, associate yourself with people who are positive. After all, you can't soar with the eagles if you constantly scratch with the turkeys. As you grow in awareness of who you really are, you will outgrow some of those who are part of your life right now who have not grown themselves.

Don't despair. Outgrowing your friends can be confusing and painful, but it is a natural part of your own personal growth. It is a necessary process. You have the right to choose to surround yourself with the people who understand you, are helpful, are compassionate, and put you at ease.

> *Great people talk about ideas. Small people talk about other people.*
> —*Tobias S. Gibson*

Perhaps months or even years into a friendship, you may find your friend is not the same person he or she once was. Perhaps the change was within them, but maybe this change has happened within you. Moving on doesn't mean that the experiences you shared together were not meaningful or important to both of you. Instead, the shift acknowledges your present needs.

Everyone who has been in your life has taught you something. There comes a time, however, to create room for those who are soon to arrive.

A Final Thought
On . . . Money
and Your Friends

In confusing or hurtful situations, be honest with those around you, say what you feel, and don't harbor anger or resentment. Share with your friends—the sooner the better—what is troubling you. If you let time pass, you become more annoyed; once the situation worsens, you explode with anger, say things that you'd prefer to keep quiet, and accomplish nothing.

If you are on the receiving end of anger, try not to be defensive. Relax, unfold your arms from across your chest, stop your unintentional frowning, and accept what is coming. Open your ears but, above all else, open your mind and heart and prepare to listen attentively. Understand that if someone is revealing something that is not pleasing to you, perhaps the person cares for you too much to keep quiet.

We all know that appearances can be deceiving. It is better to be direct and clear regarding what is affecting you so that you can get over misunderstandings and bitterness, rather than maintain a phony smile to avoid confrontation. If everyone had an open mind and was ready to listen to others' views without feeling attacked, humiliated, or persecuted, human relations would be much simpler and therapists would be far less busy.

So remember, don't let it go. State your feelings with humility, share your point of view while keeping in mind the arguments of others, and try to construct, with a positive spirit, the friendship building. That's the one that is built one brick at a time, day after day.

8

MONEY
AND
LOVE

A man is moving his piano. It's half in and half out the door to his apartment. He struggles fruitlessly as he tries to budge the unyielding contraption. Finally, a neighbor walks by and offers to help. With a sigh of relief the owner gratefully accepts. The two of them continue to struggle for another half hour without any success. At last, the owner exclaims: "It's no use. We'll never get it out!" At which point the neighbor pokes his head up quizically and says, "Out?"

The short answer to most financial problems between couples can be found in the moral of this story—it is essential to share the same goal.

You, Me, and Money Make Three

You may know his favorite song, but do you know how much money he has in his 401(k) account, how he intends to pay off his credit card debt, who will manage the family finances, or how much money each one of you could lend a friend without having to consult with the other? Do you find yourself rolling your eyes, thinking, "What does that have to do with love?" or "I trust him completely"?

You'd better pull up a chair. We need to talk.

I would never attempt to preach a formula for a perfect marriage, but considering that the cause of more than half of divorces is financial pressures, it is not presumptuous to assume that if you come into the relationship knowing how to handle, respect, and manage your partner's money style and yours, you increase the chances of celebrating your golden wedding anniversary together and in harmony. Money can be a very touchy subject in the context of love, but getting over the discomfort that prevents two committed people from discussing their finances is a critical component of your future happiness. In other words, if you communicate well about money with your partner, you may find that those skills translate into an openness that extends past finances into other serious relationship considerations.

So far in this book, I've offered some pointers on how to maximize the tendencies in your own personality to help you achieve your goals. Knowing and appreciating your natural instincts and the cause behind your ability—or inability—to make financial decisions puts you in conscious control of your life. Even your weaknesses lose their steam as soon as you become aware of them and how they undermine your goals. You may even feel so much in charge of your financial life that you begin to experiment beyond your natural boundaries and occasionally borrow some characteristics of other types, simply to see what it feels like. More power to you.

But before you can communicate with your partner about what money represents to you, it's imperative for each of you to identify your own individual reaction to making, saving, spending, and investing, because only then can you take the next step—combining both your personalities to create a partnership where nobody feels emotionally or financially wiped out. This is where it all gets quite interesting.

You may fall in love with someone quite different from yourself because you find the differences very appealing, assuming it will be a minor task to tweak what you find bothersome, leaving you with a perfect mate. In many cases, the very thing that was part of the attraction in courtship turns into the source of irritation in marriage.

When asked his secret of love, having been married for fifty-four years to the same person, Billy Graham said, "Ruth and I are happily incompatible."

For example, when you were dating, you may have found it awfully romantic to be showered with lavish gifts from your loved one without giving a second thought to where he got the funds, but once you're married and share a joint checking account, chances are you are going to resent his flamboyant spending and feel totally out of control over your own finances, not to mention your financial future together. Even if you are a Dionysian yourself, statistics show that with time, one of you is going to turn into the miser in the relationship.

Show Me Yours and I'll Show You Mine

Opposites can indeed attract. But to avoid a nasty cash clash in your own household, watch out for the three primary signs that you are headed for financial conflicts in your relationship:

1. You haven't discussed your common goals, expectations, priorities, or preferences in money management with your partner—remember the piano story.

2. You find that you have different philosophies around money issues—not a problem in itself, but things can turn chaotic if you don't know how to handle the variance.

3. One of you feels superior and wants to control the other with money.

The Now

Although there is no clear line of demarcation between the money types we have covered in this book, you may identify with one or more of the following traits that typically accompany each temperament when it comes to relationships. The following list will help you understand the natural tendencies of your partner and how to approach the conversation about money in a way that capitalizes on your partner's natural instincts. See how many of the following characteristics exemplify how you or your partner communicate:

The Diva: As a Diva, your attitude toward relationships is rather old-fashioned. The security and social status of marriage represents one more validation of your worth as a lovable human being. As a partner, you tend to be loyal, dependable, and hardworking, and you provide a solid foundation on which to build a family. Trust is very important to you.

Because you associate money with power and status, you have the highest emotional reaction to it, and your conversations about the subject are filled with emotion. You don't want to be at anyone's mercy when it comes to your money, and it is important for you to be self-sufficient and able to make spending decisions on your own. You are happiest with a comfortable degree of autonomy.

Your partner is well-advised to ask—at the very least—your opinion before taking any steps toward a major purchase. Even if you choose not to be involved in the decision making, the fact that you were consulted makes you feel validated and less likely to throw down a stormy objection.

As you learn to expand your investment horizons by moving from savings to buying shares of stocks or mutual funds, your partner's comments or words of encouragement about your investments will encourage you to increase your self-confidence and grow. Negative comments can set you back and cost you a lot of emotional ground.

The Do-Gooder: If you are a Do-Gooder, you are looking for a soul partner, not just a companion. You are imaginative, emotionally vulnerable, and full of wonder about life and love. You are an incurable romantic and may be vulnerable to the trap of avoiding money discussions until the situation is so bad that you must take action. You like to skip the small talk and mull things over on a deeper level, and you prefer subjects that connect people heart to heart. Because you are very sensitive to the feelings of those around you, you are very susceptible to the mood of your spouse. It's important for your partner to understand this about you and be ready to explain in great detail the motivation behind his actions, to keep you from missing the mark if left on your own to find the meaning behind them.

When communicating with you about money, it is best to begin at the end—that is, the big picture. For example, you will be more receptive to your partner if he says to you: "Let's run away together to that bed-and-breakfast place we love so much! We can go next weekend and use the refund money we just got from Uncle Sam." Instead of "What do you want to do with the refund?" In other words, you must be allowed to draw a mental picture before you become engaged in the conversation about how to get the funds to achieve a goal.

Since you need to be enticed to talk about money because you consider it a frivolous subject, propositions with definite end points are necessary. You need to get excited and onboard about the project before you work out the details.

The Diligent Investigator: If you are a Diligent Investigator, you inherently harbor a great deal of skepticism and ambition. You can seem tough-minded and cold at times, when all you are actually trying to do is to balance your love life and your professional life. You typically look for someone you not only love but also admire. It isn't uncommon, in spite of the deep bond you share with your partner, that you need to be reminded to get your nose out of your books or computer and come join the family. When confronted with an emotional partner, you tend to wait quietly until the anger burns itself out in the other person—something that may ignite the discussion even more if you are dealing with a Do-Gooder, a Diva, or a Dionysian, personalities who need to be heard and validated.

Since emotions add details that can befuddle you a bit, the best way for your partner to communicate with you is to offer you the plain facts and stick to the subject in simple, direct terms. Your mind works best from the part to the whole. Instead of starting a sentence with the big picture, your partner will get the point across to you better by starting with the smallest piece of the puzzle.

Your partner would be wise to find a practical reason to justify a purchase or investment since it is more important for you to understand that something is useful today rather than see the future possibilities. Once you hear your partner out, you tend to ask many questions that could be interpreted as a sign of having misgivings, when in fact, you are simply asking to satisfy your natural need for more information.

The Dionysian: Your optimism is one of your most endearing qualities. You are spontaneous, generous, and exude a playful sexuality that is very appealing to your partner. You bring a sense of fun and excitement to the relationship. You live with flair. If you are a loud one—an extrovert—you probably favor large parties with lots of friends, food, and noise. If you're an introvert, you may prefer more peaceful surroundings, but you still have a sparkle in your eye and can be quite mischievous.

Life with you can be "feast or famine" because you live so much in the present that sometimes you can't meet the financial objectives that a marriage needs in order to thrive. You need a long leash to be able to breathe. This means that your partner needs to be very tolerant of your toys, your tools, and your adventures. This is why commitment does not come easily to you.

But as your relationships turn from dating to courtship, you may want to please your partner by promising to turn over a new leaf and assume a new role, something that may work for a short time but that eventually doesn't last very long, in spite of your most sincere efforts. Budgets, long-term goals, even the word "tomorrow" are all foreign concepts to you, so your partner needs to be very careful not to use terms that will make your eyes glaze over. Things should be put in terms of "wishes" instead of, God forbid, "goals."

You can be very good with money as long as it is kept in the present. Even though you don't want to be part of the everyday budgeteering, you need to be consulted, and most of all, you need to have autonomy over money since to you, money is symbolic of love. If you have no money, you feel as if you have no love, which can make you depressed, even physically ill.

But you are no money dummy either. Your ability to communicate and inspire people makes you an excellent candidate for sales in real estate, stocks, or even insurance. As long as a plan can lead to fun and excitement, you are a willing partner, so you need to be recruited from that angle. Chances are, however, that you will forget your commitment to the plan unless you both keep it short term.

The Dependable Hoarder: You like routine and honor schedules, sticking to the tried-and-true rather than exploring new horizons. Risk is a four-letter word from which you try to stay away at any cost. This makes you a very cautious partner who tends to lord over the money subject, making you an entirely intimidating creature to approach for funds. When a family member or spouse attempts this, they'd better be prepared to explain *why* they need the money, and the explanation needs to be on a rational level rather than an emotional one.

Your budgets and projections keep you safe and within

your comfort level, so when you see an unexpected charge, you may make comments to your family that cause friction, such as, "You spent way too much money this week—what's the matter with you?" All it means to you, really, is that you budgeted for a specific amount and the actual expense has gone over it. It doesn't mean that you are judging the person who did the spending. In a conversation about money, advantages should outweigh the discomfort created by breaking the status quo. You want to keep things simple.

Your response to these statements will offer you an opportunity to engage in a dialogue about money and the role each of you plays in your financial lives. Once you understand your financial personality and your partner's learn to communicate effectively, approaching each other in terms that are most easily processed according to your natural style. When you determine your goals, you will begin to turn frustration into understanding and understanding into productive new choices.

How Do You Rate?

Now that you have explored some positive ways to communicate about money with different personality types, use the following quiz as a diagnostic tool to identify the areas that you and your partner need to consider. Answer each statement individually and then compare your answers.

Circle your response for each of the following statements:

1. My partner handles money according to the plans we have made together.

   I agree   I disagree

2. My partner and I divide our money responsibilities according to our own abilities.

   I agree   I disagree

3. I know my partner's money personality.

   I agree   I disagree

4. My partner and I know how much money we have and how much money we owe.

   I agree   I disagree

5. Money is just one more subject of conversation between my partner and me.

   I agree   I disagree

Any glaring discrepancies in answers between you and your partner should be addressed sooner rather than later.

The Future

It makes perfect sense to buy into the idea that unless you know where you're going, you're never going to get there, right? But how do you really know how to handle your list of wants and wishes when they can seem so overwhelming? Let me help you both, as individuals and as a couple, to identify a workable checklist that will simplify the process and offer you another opportunity to interact with each other in a positive way about your financial future together.

Remember the piano story at the beginning of this chapter? Here are the steps to make sure you and your partner move your piano in the same direction:

1. Make a list of ten things you would like to achieve individually. They can be related to your career, income, housing, recreation, travel, retirement, children's education, community involvement, relationship, or health. Feel free to address your physical, mental, and spiritual self.

2. Once you have your list of ten wishes, rate them in order of importance from one to ten, with one being the most important to you. Use this grading scale: items with a one, two, or three grade are those that you consider a necessity more than a wish; four and five are those items that you would like to accomplish but are more an option than a need; six through ten will be those items that represent things you would like to accomplish if possible.

3. Now go back to the list and write down how long you are willing to wait to accomplish each item.

4. Next, put a dollar sign ($) next to each item that would cost money and a heart (♥) next to the ones that feel good but won't cost money.

5. Now it's time to exchange your list with your partner.

6. Go over your partner's list, and choose two items that you are willing to help pursue. Your partner should do the same.

7. You now have communicated to each other two items that are extremely important to each of you, and you have identified four items that you are committed to reaching as a couple. Shhhhh, don't tell anyone, you have just managed to select eight goals that you are committed to reaching either personally or together. That's more than half the battle right there.

8. Your list is a work in progress, so meet on a regular basis or question each other about whether you need to adjust it if you find yourselves making decisions that would interfere with your set goals. It's okay to change the items on your list or their level of importance. What matters is that you will amend your goals together and you will both participate in the process of doing it. This simple exercise can avoid many disagreements. The purpose of making this list is to clarify in your mind what's really important to you and to develop a joint blueprint.

Look over your list. When you consider your must-reach goals, what do they have in common? Is it pleasure? Freedom? Security? Status? What about your spouse? These are powerful emotions that need to be validated.

Don't beat each other up over them. Accept them and keep them in check so they lose the power over your relationship. The only way you can disarm the unconscious mechanism

> *I got gaps; you got gaps; we fill each other's gaps.*
> —Rocky

that can erode your relationship is by being aware of your invisible beliefs about money.

Congratulations! You have just begun to move that piano in the same direction!

You Bring the Concrete, I Bring the Steel

This may not sound like a very romantic combination to you, but there's a lot to be said about the relationship between these two materials. Concrete has what is called a very high compressive quality, which means in plain English that it can withstand a lot of weight without crushing. However, if you took a long rectangular block of concrete and hit it with a heavy tool, it would crack and collapse.

Steel, on the other hand, has a very flexible strength quality. So if you lay a long piece of steel across an opening, and hit it with the same tool you used to crumble the concrete, it would either bend or maintain its original shape—it would not crack. But can you stand a steel beam on its end and have it support a very heavy weight? Chances are it would not be able to carry the load without giving in.

Each component, on its own, has both a strength and a

weakness. But here comes the interesting part. When you combine steel with concrete, the end result is reinforced concrete—a powerful combination to be reckoned with. The result of this happy marriage is a material that is far stronger than either concrete or steel could ever dream of being. The final product has the strengths of both without the weaknesses of either.

A romantic partnership can work the same way. If each person understands his unique strengths and weaknesses, he can work with his partner to literally *join forces,* which will naturally capitalize on each of their strengths. Sort of one plus one equals eleven, rather than two.

Most couples deal with their confusion concerning money by doing nothing about it, turning the subject into a weapon to either conquer or manipulate each other. In that case, both lose. Break the pattern and take your life out of automatic pilot. You may feel that everyone else shares the secret of how to do things right. Well, if that's the case, I am about to liberate you and give you permission to carve your own path.

When it comes to money, there is no right or wrong way to do things. Since marriage is a team sport, the ultimate goal is to do what feels right to both of you: If you have a personal need for autonomy, discuss it with your partner and keep "his," "hers," and "ours" accounts—regardless of what your parents did or didn't do. You can accomplish this by adding up your monthly expenses and depositing that amount, plus a little extra, into the joint account and keeping the difference in your personal ones. If you have trouble deciding what to do with your retirement money, open individual retirement accounts for each of you and make it a fun project to see who does better using the investment style that feels most comfortable.

If you are risk averse and your partner is a gambler in the market, agree to take 10 percent of an account and invest it more aggressively. Here is a foolproof system I saw put into action by a couple that just couldn't get a grip on their spending. They told me they called it the "half-hour rule," and it works like this:

1. They divided their take-home pay by forty to get their hourly take-home pay rate.
2. Next, they allocated one half hour's worth of their salary per day to their retirement account, one half hour's worth to pay off debt, and a half hour's worth per day for an emergency account. These add up to seven and one half hours per week.
3. After they paid their monthly expenses, they indulged in using any leftover money any way they wished. By breaking down their money to thirty-minute increments, this couple learned to budget themselves and adopt a plan that they could live with. Their savings grew and their debts decreased . . . along with their disagreements about money management.

I thought their plan was brilliant, mainly because *they* thought their plan was brilliant. They continued to apply their model, no matter how much they earned per week. Let go of your power trips around money. Take responsibility for your own happiness by learning how to maneuver around your temperament and your partner's. Don't expect your spouse to read your mind. Tell him what you need to hear and how you need to hear it. Have fun with it, lighten up already!

> When the grass looks greener on the other side of the fence, it may be that they take better care of it there.
> —Cecil Selig

After all has been said and done, do you know what studies have shown about men, women, and money? That both men and women agree on one thing: they'd prefer that their partner spend more time, not money, on them. Go figure!

A *Final Thought On* . . . *Money and Love*

Everything that can be said about a particular couple will always and invariably be based on the love that is shared and expressed between them. Without love, there is no possibility for a couple to walk the marvelous path of happiness and fulfillment. Don't allow a routine lifestyle to control your destiny. This poses one of the most serious dangers for a couple. Ask yourself often, "Do I choose to marry you?" and wait for the answer. As soon as you realize that all is not going as smoothly as before, remedy the situation before it is too late.

Just as important as the previous question is this one: "If I were my spouse, would I stay?" Ask yourself this periodically and be truthful with your answer. Rediscover with time those events that you both enjoyed while dating: memories of a candlelit dinner, a romantic weekend getaway, or a rose for no apparent reason. For a couple, the most effective preventive medicine is a few days to themselves, without children, newspapers, or office calls.

Do not fear crises. A crisis means change, and through changes we grow, learn, and become stronger. Apart from not fearing them, confront them along with your partner with love, respect, and open ears, and hearts primed to sincerely understand what is affecting the other, to perceive what he or she is feeling. A couple that does not face difficulty once in a while runs a greater risk of succumbing to boredom and paralysis, compared to another couple that tackles adversity with love and courage and is always concerned for each other. Recognizing that solving a conflict single-handedly is impossible is just as important as asking for assistance at the appropriate moment. The quicker you decide to act, the better it is.

Respecting individual needs without distancing oneself from the joy of being together is a major challenge for any couple. Set aside your selfishness and you will see a synergistic, upward-spiral movement. When one comprehends and accepts the needs of the other (and vice versa), the maturity of both in all aspects of life will flourish naturally. With such an attitude, the couple will be together but not bound, connected even if separated.

A couple that is the result of two people without common interests or goals can be frustrated, distressed, and devastated. The same can happen when individualism is lost to the extent that there is no differentiation. Liven up—seek and maintain ways to balance your life. Whatever happens, if you still feel deep in your soul the love of your partner, if the passion still burns, then keep trying—it's never too late!

9

MONEY
AND
GETTING
OLDER

Jerry looked across the counter at his wife, Joan. She was shaping croquettes and laughing at a joke their daughter, Stephanie, had made about their catering clients. His heart swelled with love and contentment; he adored his beautiful wife more today than when they got married.

But, goodness, she was looking a bit old these days. Those laugh lines! The crow's-feet! Jerry looked down at his own hands as they piped crème into pastry and laughed at himself too. Of course he recognized these hands, but when on earth had they become so lined? When would they take on the crepe-paper texture so common to *old* men? Jerry shook his head and assured himself, "Very soon, very soon indeed."

Joan glanced over at her handsome husband. Oh no, he was mumbling to the dessert again! Jerry wasn't elderly, by any means, so why did he display the early signs of dementia? His behavior didn't exactly make her feel like a spring chicken. After all, she was the elder of the two by several months. She would have to boldly step into her (gulp) fifties in three weeks. And that loon over there having conversations with his spatula would get to stay forty-nine!

Joan knew she feared aging; there was so much to be

scared of. Not just the gray hairs and the support under-garments, but the growing dread of the financial responsi-bilities that lay ahead of them. Their catering business was reasonably successful, they worked like dogs and had al-ways been very frugal, but recent events had started to ac-celerate the graying of hairs and need for supportive undergarments. Supportive anything, really. Joan was torn between funneling money to the growing needs of her and Jerry's aging parents and the typical demands of a teenage daughter.

Jerry's dad had passed away five years ago, and since then, his mother has lived by herself in another part of the country where Jerry's younger brother lives. She remains very active in her church activities and travels frequently with the ladies in her parish. Financially, Jerry's mother receives a pension from her previous employer as well as her husband's retirement.

Joan's parents, on the other hand, have lived with them since her dad suffered a stroke that left him unable to care for himself. Joan's mother stays home with her husband, and they've hired an assisting nurse who visits on a daily basis to help with Dad. Joan's mother's monthly income consists of a check from Social Security and a small pen-sion from her husband. The proceeds from the sale of their home provide an additional money stream that helps pay for the medical bills.

Even though Joan and Jerry started a college fund for Stephanie years ago, the deposits they swore they'd make regularly have been discontinued on more than one occasion due to the frequent strains on their cash flow—such as the special bed for Dad to make it easier for him to get up and lie down, as well as the cost of widening doorways to accommodate his wheelchair.

Aside from the emotional trauma associated with seeing their parents age, Joan and Jerry's financial concerns go beyond their personal need to invest for their own retirement. Even though they feel confident that they have prepared for unforeseen events such as illness and death with adequate health and life insurance coverage, Joan and Jerry are now very concerned about the possibility of a lingering convalescence for either of them. That scenario could result in not only a strain on their family's income, but also additional emotional consequences they have not prepared to overcome.

How Could It All Get So Complicated?

This is a typical case of good news, bad news. The good news is that we are living longer. A sixty-five-year-old retiring today is expected to live another sixteen to nineteen years, on average. The bad news is that those years are not necessarily productive or spent in good health. And unfortunately, the news doesn't get much better for society as a whole. In the next thirty years, the number of older Americans will continue to grow at an accelerating rate. In 2000,

A Thought Exercise

In the course of attempting to come up with a meaningful career path, guidance counselors often ask young adults what they would do all day if they didn't have to work for the rest of their lives. You have the opportunity to reinvent yourself after retirement. Spend a few hours playing, imagining, and brainstorming; your dreams will help lead you in the direction of the financial goals you need to set.

4.2 million Americans were eighty-five or older. By 2030, nearly 9 million Americans will be over that age.

With this reality looming, it is obvious that our financial planning needs to include strategies for the care of our parents. Add to this the responsibility of planning for our own future needs, to provide ourselves with the services we will need to maintain our dignity and autonomy in our old age.

Redefining the Word "Retirement"

When you read the word "retirement," what comes to your mind? For me, it used to mean leaving the workforce for good, a sustained vacation for the rest of my life. But after the rather appealing notion of sleeping in every day if I choose, my idea of what retirement really means becomes rather blurry. Do I get to live happily ever after? Will I be forced to go fishing? What if I don't want to babysit the grandchildren every afternoon? I've never been terribly fond of rocking chairs. So, what's the deal with modern retirement? And what does my financial personality have to say about it? Of all the chapters in this book, this one actually hinges the least on your financial personality. What you choose to do during your later years is a personality issue; taking the necessary steps today to ensure that the money exists later is a universal one.

Today's retirement vision is different from those of our parents and grandparents. Many workers who are approaching retirement age are planning to continue working. Many successful managers become consultants or contract workers, "laboring" within a flexible schedule that suits their new lifestyle. In other words, the new retiree is not necessarily looking for a quiet corner in which to grow old; he's looking for a spiritually and physically stimulating environment where he still matters. And studies show that retirees who continue to work or volunteer, or people who delay retirement, have more meaningful latter years. They live longer than their peers who choose to celebrate their retirement from the workforce by turning on their televisions and silently awaiting their retirement from life.

The fact that there will be fewer younger workers to replace retirees due to a decrease in population will translate into more opportunities for employment for older retirees. So, what if instead of asking you about your retirement, I were to ask you about planning for your older age, planning for a time, perhaps the first time in your entire life, when you get to call the shots 100 percent? Does that sound more relevant? It certainly does to me—and statistically, to a lot of other people.

Not Winding Down, Just Rewinding

As the baby boomers (those born between the years of 1946 and 1964) reach their sixties, they may be looking at sitting down, but it will most likely be on a Harley rather than in a wheelchair. These post–World War II babies represent about one third of the U.S. population, and their unwillingness to go gentle into that good night is redefining the term "old age."

So, the question becomes: What should you be doing *today* to practically, physically, psychologically, and financially prepare yourself for the future, and how does your temperament help or hinder your readiness for a golden age filled with meaningful and satisfying experiences?

The Employee Benefit Research Institute (EBRI) found that your personality type and your attitude toward financial and retirement savings can directly affect how well prepared you will be for your old age.

The Diva: Has a "doing" temperament where money management means having the freedom to do what feels good at the time and to make an impression. This type is good at tactics, reading the immediate situation, and can make instant decisions to accomplish a limited, short-term purpose. Not as helpful when we're thinking long-term.

The Diva has the ability to make the right financial adjustments to deal with unforeseen circumstances. In other words, if he has the money, he spends it; if he doesn't have it, he finds the way to get it. This personality type can't tell you how much money he has in his retirement account. His busy lifestyle and lack of personal interest in finances places planning for the future in the "should do" list, which somehow never gets done. His haphazard savings may be used for an emerging opportunity or a spur-of-the-minute purchase rather than a well-thought-out plan of action. He expects to work during his old age, anyway.

The Do-Gooder: Has an "inspiring" temperament. Money management is about cultivating relationships, growing personally, and helping others achieve their potential. In retirement planning, Do-Gooders are naturally altruistic and willing to substantially sacrifice themselves to the betterment of others—a quality that proves to be counterproductive in planning for their financial independence in old age.

Because they have a general apathy about money, Do-Gooders usually have a fragile financial foundation and poor preparation for the future. They are not usually interested in the accumulation of wealth. For money to matter to them, it must maintain integrity with their personal ethics, moral standards, and ideals. The Do-Gooder feels it's pointless to plan for retirement because it's too far away, anyhow.

The Diligent Investigator: This temperament has an "achieving" purpose. For him, money management is about acquiring the necessary competence to understand, explain, predict, and control his life—handy, if it were possible to do all of these things without a time machine or a psychic. He's skilled in strategy and long-range plans. It isn't a surprise then that this personality is more likely to have saved money for retirement.

Diligent Investigators rate the highest in the accumulation of money and the earlier retirement categories among all personality types. He is very involved in the planning because of his natural orientation toward the future and his ability to be a big-picture thinker. However, studies show that the only regret of the Diligent Investigator at retirement time is the wish to have started investing sooner and taken more risks.

The Dionysian: This temperament is usually impulsive, bold, and overly optimistic. He is inclined to take financial risks that can propel or crumble his chances to amass any considerable amount of money. A Dionysian would much rather trust his instincts than be limited by detailed financial plans about the future or financial statements about his present fiscal condition. He would rather lose money than miss out on an opportunity to make money. What is the Dionysian's attitude toward retirement? "Who has money to invest for retirement? I'm lucky if I can pay my bills this month! Social Security will take care of me." Risky.

The Dependable Hoarder: This personality type doesn't tend to prepare for a sunny retirement; instead, he prepares for a rainy day, a time when he can no longer continue to work and generate income. He has a "preserving" attitude toward money. He has contingent what-if plans for the future. The emphasis is usually on making sure that the money is being managed "right" by following the rules of frugal spending, saving money, minimizing debt, and preparing for any possible doom in the future. The protection of his family is very important to a Dependable Hoarder, so insurance coverage is usually in place.

This type can set up definite retirement goals and methodically work toward them with self-discipline.

Everything I Need to Know (About Retirement) I Learned from *The Golden Girls*

The Diva: Blanche Devereaux. Typical Diva, she buys a big house she cannot afford and is forced to take in boarders. Lucky for us! Blanche's lesson is that there is life after the death of a spouse, if we choose to embrace him. I mean, it. Embrace *it*.

The Do-Gooder: Rose Nylund. She believes in honesty, she believes in love, she believes in her friends, but mostly, she believes in the power of a shared cheesecake to fix a broken world. She teaches us that we don't need to fear getting older, as long as we remain true to what we are. Especially if what we are is adorably kooky.

The Dependable Hoarder: Dorothy Petrillo-Zbornak. How else to explain the sensible flats and protective shoulder pads? Dorothy teaches us to be smart, to be on our toes, and to gracefully opt out of poorly executed sitcom sequels. Did anyone ever watch *The Golden Palace*?

The Dionysian: Sophia Petrillo. Waste away at Shady Pines? Never! This wise lady may look delicate, but she has a serious appetite for life. Sophia shows the world that the older members of the community are to be respected—and not just a little feared.

The Diligent Investigator: Stan Zbornak. Always investigating ways to manipulate the women, he is a beacon of indecision and false starts. Stan's lesson to us? Don't wear a toupee.

Money equals security, peace of mind, comfort (not luxury), and a sense of well-being. He wants to be ready for any emergency that can occur. A Dependable Hoarder needs to put aside a larger amount of money because the lower return on his savings, taxes, and inflation take a toll on his retirement nest egg. He counts on Social Security and his ability to scale down his standard of living during his retirement to control costs and survive.

Are You On Track for Your Retirement?

In my many years of practice, I've had to restrain older investors, usually Divas and Dionysians, from risking their money too aggressively when they realize, close to retirement, that what they have put aside is simply not enough, and they find themselves on a desperate mission to make up for lost time. And even those who did manage to put some money aside toward retirement are worried that their nest eggs will run out before they die.

 The common mistakes among retiring savers who fall short in their retirement financial needs are usually the following:

1. Starting too late.

2. Not knowing how much money they needed to have available during retirement.

3. Lack of knowledge of investment options.

4. Holding on to losing investments too long.

Here is a simple test to help you gauge if you are on track for your later years. It should give you a good indication of your preparedness for retirement.

If you answered "I agree" to three or more statements,

186

Indicate whether you agree or disagree with the following statements:

1. My retirement plan includes investments that will keep up with inflation and are suited to my tax bracket.

   I agree   I disagree

2. I consider myself more of an investor than a saver.

   I agree   I disagree

3. I know the monthly amount I will need to be able to stop working and still enjoy life.

   I agree   I disagree

4. I know how much money I need to invest on a monthly basis to reach my retirement goal based on the returns on my investments.

   I agree   I disagree

5. I have taken the necessary steps in planning for retirement by having death and disability protection for my family.

   I agree   I disagree

you are on your way to "buying" the freedom, dignity, and options that old age brings. If you disagreed with three or more statements, I sincerely recommend that you begin to trace and follow a plan today. Let me help you do that.

Recipe for a Successful Golden Age

Just because your personality type tends to postpone retirement planning or ignores it altogether, that's no excuse to continue the tradition. You can snap out of automatic pilot and intercept your negative tendencies by following a painless and rather simple plan.

Here is a guide to assist you along the way:

Request a Statement of Benefits from Social Security: Although we don't know with certainty what your Social Security benefits will be when you retire, it is in your best interest to find out if you have met the minimum requirements for a monthly check at retirement age. Throughout your working years, based on your earnings, and varying depending on your date of birth, you receive credits toward your retirement earnings. The maximum number of credits that you are eligible to receive per calendar year is four. You need a minimum of forty credits to qualify for a Social Security check. A record of your earnings history and an estimate of how much you and your employer paid in Social Security taxes can be requested from the Web site (www.ssa.gov); they also send annual statements. At this site, you will also be able to fill out an online form to receive an estimate of the benefits you and your family may be eligible for now and in the future.

Have a clear idea of how much money you will need during retirement: To calculate how much income you will need on a monthly basis at retirement, begin by listing your monthly expenses today. Next, cross out those that you do not expect to have during retirement (it could be transportation expenses, a mortgage payment, etc.).

If you wish to have an idea of how much money you will need to set aside in the future, you can use the rule of thumb many financial planners offer: $300,000 in the bank generating $1,000 in monthly income that you require. This amount assumes that you receive a 4 percent return on your money and that you do not touch the principal amount, only the interest.

However, there is nothing verboten about using your own funds if they last as long as you need them. You may use some of that $300,000 in your account in addition to the interest the money generates. You just need to be aware of how long your money will last according to the amount you withdraw. On page 186 is a nifty table that will show you how that works.

Let's assume that you have that $300,000 in an account earning 4 percent per year. The interest will be $12,000 ($300,000 times 4 percent). Are you with me so far? Since $12,000 is your yearly interest, if you divide that figure by 12, you will get the monthly interest; in this case that number is $1,000. Since you are withdrawing the same amount as the interest earned in your account, the $300,000 will just sit there, without going up or down.

But what if instead of receiving $1,000 per month, you want to receive $1,250 ($15,000 per year) and you are still

How Many Years Will Your Money Last?

Yearly withdrawal	Yearly return on your account							
	4%	5%	6%	7%	8%	9%	10%	11%
5%	41 yrs.							
6%	28	36 yrs.						
7%	21	25	33 yrs.					
8%	17	20	23	30 yrs.				
9%	15	16	18	22	28 yrs.			
10%	13	14	15	17	20	26 yrs.		
11%	11	12	13	15	16	19	24 yrs.	
12%	10	11	12	13	14	16	18	23 yrs.

earning 4 percent on your $300,000? Well, your account would still be generating $12,000 a year. The amount of $15,000 a year would represent $3,000 more than your in-

terest, so that money has to come from the actual $300,000.
Right?

"You mean I would be chipping away at my nest egg?"
you indignantly say to me. Yes, you would, but look here,
$15,000 represents 5 percent of $300,000 (all I did was divide $15,000 by $300,000). Now take a look at the table on
page 186 and find 5 percent in the left column. Now find
4 percent in the top row (that's the interest earned). The
box where the two numbers meet is the number of years
your account will last if you withdraw 5 percent while you
are earning only 4 percent. In this case, the answer is 41
years. So, if you begin to withdraw $1,250 per month
($15,000 yearly) when you are 60 years old, you would re-
ceive your last monthly check of $1,250 at age 101!

Now for the bonus question! If you want to have your
account last until age 75, and you start using the money at
age 60, can you figure out how much you could withdraw
each month if you are still earning 4 percent? Let me get
you started: Your money would have to last you 15 years
(75 minus 60), so find the column under 4 percent and locate the square with 15 years in it. Now look at the left-
hand side of the same row. What number do you see? You
should see 9 percent. Multiplying $300,000 by 9 percent
equals $27,000. That's the yearly amount you could with-
draw. To get the answer to my question, just divide $27,000
by 12. The final number is a monthly check of $2,250. If
this is the number you got, high five to you.

But wait a minute. What if you can get more than 4 percent on your account—how long would your money last? If you could earn 8 percent on your $300,000, your money would provide you with the yearly $27,000 for 28 years. I hope you can see that by adjusting the earnings on your account, you can not only receive a higher income, but you can also extend the period of time you can count on that income. This is why it pays to learn to invest.

The bottom line is this: If you don't have a goal, you are prone to fall victim to the stereotypes of old age and the shortcomings of your own temperament. If your eyes glazed over during the previous exercise and you needed to take a coffee break before continuing to read, then find a financial planner who can do all the dirty work of number crunching for you. However, no matter who helps you with the details you abhor, remember that it is *your life, your money, and your time* we are talking about here. If you provide your planner with the amount of money you will need on a monthly (or yearly) basis now and during retirement, you will have a better chance of reaching that goal and controlling your own destiny with the dignity you deserve.

But our work together in getting you ready for a carefree retirement is not done yet. So far, we have begun to prepare to provide a stream of income for you. There are three other issues you need to discuss and decide while you have time to consider your options:

Life insurance: The first one is life insurance. "Urgh!" Yes, I know. This is usually not at the top of your list, but have you thought about what would happen to your family if you or your spouse were not there to provide for them? Would they need to sell your home or stop going to school to meet their financial obligations? Do you need to provide for a disabled child or parent who will depend on your financial support indefinitely?

When you are buying life insurance, you are in essence buying the time you need to accumulate assets. If you have implemented a financial plan based on definite goals, which you plan to reach by a certain age, good for you, but who can guarantee you that you will be there to see it come to fruition? A life insurance policy can provide your family with the security of knowing that they will be taken care of if you should pass away before achieving your goals.

There are many different kinds of life insurance policies and their explanation goes beyond the scope of this book, but I strongly recommend that you consult with your family insurance agent or financial planner about the options that suit your particular needs.

Consider a long-term care insurance policy: As life expectancy tables are stretching to astronomical lengths, the fact that we are living well into our eighties and nineties practically necessitates making allowances for future assistance with the activities of daily living, such as bathing, ambulating, feeding, etc.

With the aging of the baby boomers, there is a movement away from isolating the elderly in gruesome, cold nursing homes, and toward bringing senior citizens into more of a community atmosphere. Whether that means assisted living facilities and retirement communities that engage older persons mentally and emotionally, or the move back to home care, in the coming years you will see more products and services aimed at satisfying the needs of the aging masses. Home-delivered meals, nursing, and assisted living services will increase, and along with all other health care, the price tag of those amenities can be expected to increase as well.

If your nest egg is sizable, you can afford to pay an army to care for your safety, health, and comfort. But if you are like the majority of Americans who fall somewhere between the poor and the extremely wealthy, you need to look into a long-term care policy that will cover the cost of your independence in your old age. Your insurance agent can also provide you with the options available to you in this area. Make sure you address this issue as part of your retirement planning.

Take care of your estate: And now, we need to address your estate. "My what? I wish! I don't have an estate!" is the usual, amused answer I get from clients. Well, not so fast, buddy. If you own or owe anything, you do have an estate—and you need to take care of it unless you want the government to decide what happens.

At the very least, you need to consider having a will or a

trust, in which you give instructions for how you want your possessions to be distributed. It can be as short as a single written sentence or as complex as a hundred-page manual. Your assets may or may not have a very high monetary value, but believe me, you will be sparing emotional grief for those left behind if you leave clear instructions of your wishes. I have seen unprepared acquaintances' hard-earned money and property end up with their daughter-in-law's second husband. You can avoid the conflicts and chaos that can be created among family members and friends by simply taking care of a few details now.

Power of attorney: You also need to address a document that will give someone legal access to your financial information and those accounts that are in your name exclusively. This is called a power of attorney. This legal paper designates a person to manage and make decisions concerning your individual accounts, such as IRAs, 401(k)s, or any other type of asset that is held only in your name.

Health care directive: And lastly, you need to decide who will step into your shoes as your legal representative to carry out your health instructions and make any necessary medical decisions should you not be in a position to do it for yourself. This is the purpose of a health care directive.

If you have aging parents, make sure you discuss these issues with them too. You will find that they have been worrying about it and that it is more difficult for you to discuss it than it is for them.

Looking Ahead vs. Looking Back

Your retirement nest egg represents a lot more than a running tally of how much money you have and what profit or loss you have achieved on your investments over time. It's the symbol of your peace of mind, a salient reminder of your ability to age with dignity, without being a burden to anybody else.

But your golden years are about much more than just "preserving" what you have. It's the opportunity to engage in what really matters—your mission in life. It's a chance to give back for all the blessings you have received. And with your continuing contribution to society, you continue to grow.

Money does not equal happiness. It may not buy you health, but it does buy you options. And don't let anybody kid you otherwise. During your golden years, you have earned the right to please yourself and gained the wisdom not to judge others. With a couple of dollars in your pocket, your mature years can be the most satisfying of your life. And regardless of what your personality type is, prudent and wise planning for later years can become a harmonious component of your life today. All it takes is the willingness to become aware of possible scenarios, hoping for the best, and preparing for the unexpected.

A *Final Thought On . . .*
Money and Getting Older

Contemplate your present situation through the wisdom of your living years, setting aside any feelings of resentment, melancholy, or bitterness. Don't pay attention to what you lack or what you can no longer do. On the contrary, be grateful for all you have and the opportunity to accomplish many other tasks that await you. Take advantage of this new reality to approach postponed projects, complete unfinished activities, and fully enjoy what you have now. Within you are the scars of countless battles you have waged, and the sum total of your successes and your failures. You are alive, awake, and ready to continue honoring life after sixty with an intensity that you did not have at forty.

Do you recall everything that you had to put off? Those were times when the priorities were focused on school, work, starting a family, doing household chores, and taking care of the children—funding their education and preparing them for the future. That future is here now. Life is a double-edged sword. The good part is that "the children" have grown and are responsible for their lives, with freedom to make their own decisions. On the other hand, and with some trepidation, you feel as if they no longer need you. Don't be mistaken. Although it's certain that you are no longer as important on an hourly basis, you will realize that your contributions are much more valuable than before.

You are the one with the power to decide how to live. Each one of us makes his or her path, and halfway along the trip is when one begins to look backward, not just ahead. Forging onward is joyful when you realize the moments that alternately changed and marked the road will carry you ahead. Do you see how everything seems to fit into place, like a virtual and dynamic crossword puzzle that continues to change as it grows, adjusting itself to the meaning you give to life? Take advantage of your experience and use it. Start harvesting the fruits of the seeds you planted. Spoil your grandchildren. Allow yourself to discover new interests, or to dust off those that have been put away. Do it now—you still have time.

When your body tells you not to engage in sports and action, accept in good cheer the message and listen to what your body, mind, and spirit have to offer. You have the blessing of being alive; enjoy it to the fullest and live every day with enthusiasm, assessing who you are. As you open your eyes each morning, ask what you desire for that day, and do it.

From birth to age eighteen, a girl needs good parents.
From eighteen to thirty-five, she needs good looks.
From thirty-five to fifty-five, she needs a good personality,
and from fifty-five on, she needs good cash.
—*Sophie Tucker*

The
Realities

10

THE FEAR
OF
SUCCESS

It was the third time in a month that Maria was awakened by her husband. Again, she found herself standing in front of her dresser, staring at the open drawer. It was three in the morning.

Maria shook her head in disbelief and turned around to look at her husband, who was watching her from their bed with a puzzled and worried look on his face. She was embarrassed by these sleepwalking incidents, by the bizarre dreams that compelled them—so out of character for someone as optimistic as Maria.

They always began the same way; she was in a room of her home, busy doing something she could not exactly describe, when she heard a voice in distress from another part of the house. She hurried to the place where the sounds were coming from, and when she entered the room she saw it: a blonde doll, stuffed in the open top drawer of her dresser with a rope around its neck, half dead, only able to make that awful gurgling sound that made Maria's skin crawl. In her dream, Maria would run to the doll and pick her up with both hands, trying desperately to untie the rope but unable to find the way to do it. Maria was sobbing now, fumbling in vain to save the doll from her death. Then she would hear her husband's voice, getting closer to her, calling her name. Maria would wake up, trembling, still unconvinced that what she'd just experienced was only a dream.

Slowly, still feeling her racing heart beating painfully in her chest, Maria would return to her husband's side. "Another bad dream?" he would ask, clearly worried. "Yes, must be something I ate," she would reply. And they would kiss good night again and try to catch the last few hours of sleep before it was time to get up and begin their day.

Maria was a successful financial planner. She and her husband, Ben, ran a thriving retirement planning firm near their home in California. After more than ten years of marriage, a beautiful home, and a healthy, happy family, Maria and Ben were beginning to see the fruits of their hard work. Neither of them had come from money. They had met while working for the same company and soon realized that they shared a passion for their careers and for each other. Within a short period of time, their lives were personally and professionally entwined, and they began a business together.

Ben was the primary breadwinner, while Maria's skills were used in an administrative capacity. They complemented each other in a way that made their business very successful in a very short period of time. After a while, their professional roles had begun to reverse. In order to expand their practice, Maria had begun offering free financial planning seminars for women in local libraries and schools. She kept the meetings concise and entertaining, showing her audience how to solve a practical financial dilemma—how to choose the best fund within a retirement plan, or how to discover and purchase a good stock with ease.

The meetings became wildly popular in a few months, and the attendees wanted more. So, she helped those who were interested to form investment clubs where they could begin to practice their newly found skills with very little money and in a welcoming social atmosphere. Before long, a reporter came to one of the meetings and was taken aback by the enthusiastic reaction of the participants; she wrote a glowing article in the newspaper. That article changed Maria's life forever.

Maria was shocked at the immediacy of her success. There were requests from all over the country for speaking engagements; there was a book offer, a television pilot, and soon Maria found herself the focus of a lot of unexpected attention. It was all very exciting . . . and terribly scary.

She found her personal life was changing too. As Maria's fame became more apparent, she began to take overnight trips for television interviews. Ben would stay home, taking care of the business and their son. Tensions began to build as the couple struggled to redefine their roles both in business and at home. Someone was rocking the boat. Was it worth it? And what did this haunting dream have to do with it?

Will the Real Maria Please Stand Up?

I am Maria, and this is my story.

Shortly after these uncomfortable episodes, I went to a psychologist to try to understand what was happening to me. I knew that something was bothering me, but what? I was happily married, and I loved my family and my job. Why couldn't I just enjoy the journey?

I was familiar with failure—most of us are, in some way or another. And for the most part, it didn't scare me. I wasn't one to crumble under the possibility of not succeeding. In fact, I didn't even know what I was trying to accomplish. And that was the first clue! I learned that I wasn't afraid of having to deal with failure. I was scared stiff of having to deal with success!

That little doll was really me, crying out of fear of not being heard, of drowning, stuffed in that drawer. I was afraid of not being loved anymore, of breaking unspoken rules of conduct. I was afraid of being left behind while I raced forward. Crazy? I thought so too . . . until I understood.

I had felt this way once before.

When I was in college, I had a part-time job as a teacher's assistant in an elementary school. I was in my senior year, one semester away from receiving an Elementary Teaching Credential, when I was given my student teaching assignment. I went on the teaching requirement for a few weeks to a school under the direct supervision of a "master teacher." Student teaching is supposed to bring all the theoretical lessons you have learned to a practical level, an apprentice period where you get to try out what you have learned, from lesson plans to visual aids to actual class control, lesson delivery, and methods of evaluating your results. It was a very scary proposition for me.

I had wanted to be a teacher ever since I could remember. And now that I was a few months away from my goal, I didn't want to go through with it. I found all kinds of excuses why I should go into business, accounting, or something related to the world of entrepreneurs instead. My new line of thinking came as a shock to my family, my counselors, and me.

I mentioned my plans to leave the education field to the teacher in my part-time job. She told me that she was very surprised to hear me say that, especially because she saw that I truly seemed to enjoy being around the children. She looked me straight in the eyes and asked: "What are you afraid of?"

The question took me completely by surprise and, almost without thinking, I answered her: "I'm afraid of teaching." To which she casually replied, "Julie, you have to go to the place you fear the most." And with that, she grabbed her whistle and called the class in from physical education to line up. No more discussions, just a simple statement that has stayed with me the rest of my life. I did stick it out, finished my student teaching with flying colors, and became a first-grade teacher the same year I graduated from school. I loved my job.

Now the same familiar feelings of inadequacy were back. And this time they were back with a vengeance. Why did I seem to want to sabotage myself just when

> *Failure is a trickster with a keen sense of irony and cunning. It takes great delight in tripping one when success is almost within reach.*
> —Napoleon Hill

I got to the doorway that was to take me somewhere exciting and where I could find the opportunity to continue growing? Why was I so scared?

What Is Fear of Success?

Most of you are familiar with the fear of failure: looking at the future with an apprehension based on your past. *Fear of failure is the fear of not reaching your goals and being unhappy as a result.*

It is not easy to overcome the fear of failure. People who are successful at it have the ability ask themselves honestly, "What is the worst thing that could happen?" and then mentally proceed through that scenario, gradually realizing that if indeed the worst did take place, it wouldn't be the end of the world, and they are able to move on from that point.

Fear of success, on the other hand, is looking forward, imagining what will happen once you enter truly unknown territory. *Fear of success is the fear that you will reach your goals and continue being unhappy in spite of it.* And that is a very real fear indeed!

The fear of success is wound up in the fear that you will be punished for violating the stereotypes of your environment, your family, the traditional roles of your sex, and your community standards. It's that little voice inside of you asking you: "And just who do you think *you* are?"

> *Life shrinks or expands in proportion to one's courage.*
> —Anaïs Nin

In 1916, Sigmund Freud wrote an essay called "Those Wrecked by Success," about "the surprising and ever bewildering" tendency of some people to fall apart "precisely when a deeply rooted and long-cherished wish has come to fulfillment . . . as though they were not able to tolerate happiness." It appears, according to him and scores of other psychologists, that we tend to snatch defeat from the jaws of victory.

Seems silly, doesn't it? After all, if you find yourself on the other side of the fence, looking in at success, you might wonder how anyone could possibly fear such a wonderful positive thing.

Do You Have a Secret?

You may be holding on to a secret image of yourself, and the possibility of having to change that self-image—even if it's for the better—can trigger feelings of fear and inadequacy. You will achieve only the level of success that your image of yourself can absorb. And sometimes that takes time.

The roots of these feelings, according to psychologists, can come from long ago, if during your childhood someone you admired or deeply cared for convinced you that you weren't very smart or very competent or very likable or that nothing you did was ever quite good enough. If that happened, the theory goes, you will have a very hard time believing that you *are* capable of doing well in life or, even wilder, that you *deserve* to.

You emit constant, unconscious clues as to how you view yourself in the course of a day. Try this: For the next day or so, watch your language. Specifically, watch the words you use to refer to yourself. How many times during the course of a day do you put yourself down? Run a tally. You'll probably be surprised at how hard on yourself you really are.

Are You Suffering from Fear of Success?

This is a quiz based on several assessments. Take it to find out if you are your own best friend or your worst enemy.

Read each of the following statements and either agree or disagree:

1. I frequently find myself not telling others about my successes in order to avoid envy.

   I agree   I disagree

2. Others say I'm smart, funny, and capable, but I tend to have a low opinion of myself.

   I agree   I disagree

3. I feel guilty when I say no to other people.

   I agree   I disagree

4. When things seem to be going well, I get scared, as if I'm waiting for the other shoe to drop.

   I agree   I disagree

5. I generally feel guilty about my own happiness if a friend tells me that s(he)'s depressed.

   I agree   I disagree

If you answered "I agree" to three or more statements, you may be starving for success and it may be there, if only you could get out of your own way.

Success Comes with Fallout

It might seem very silly to you, on the surface, to conceive of anyone consciously avoiding success. And you're right. The fear of success is very often an unconscious reaction. It can manifest itself in different ways: a migraine headache forcing you to cancel a much-anticipated date, laryngitis right before a vocal performance, staying up late and exhausting yourself the night before an important exam, or forgetting where you put a vital document. Have any of these ever happened to you?

Why then would we consciously or unconsciously avoid something as sweet as success? Here are a few of the powerful reasons:

• Envy: The unpleasant knowledge that people are jealous of you can be terribly off-putting. If you are prettier, smarter, make more money, are more popular, etc. than your friends, they may resent you and reject you. You may leave former peers behind, symbolically and literally. Many will feel happy for your success, and others may feel envious. Coping with these attitudes, especially from those whom you love, can be a very daunting process.

211

- Facing the unfamiliar: A routine, even when unpleasant, can be reassuring. Success brings change, and change means having to adjust. If you change, all those around you need to change as well. Life can seem simpler when you can live it on autopilot. Change can bring exciting adventures and scary possibilities.
- Raising the expectations of others: You may feel you got away with it once, but you may not be able to keep it up. Perhaps you attribute your success to luck rather than allowing the credit you really deserve to be internalized.
- Your own negative interpretation of successful people: If you think that success means you're craftier or slicker than others, then success may be perceived as frightening and negative.
- Being "found out": You may be afraid to have other people "know" that you are faking it. This comes from your fear that you may not be as great as others think you are.

"Our deepest fear is not that we are inadequate. It is our light, not our darkness, that most frightens us. We ask ourselves, Who am I to be brilliant, gorgeous, talented, fabulous? Actually, who are you not to be?"
—*Marianne Williamson*

- Lack of belief that you can sustain your progress: You may feel that it can all go away overnight and that you will not be able to maintain the level of performance expected of you.
- Feeling selfish and self-centered: If you feel better about yourself when you are helping other people pursue their dreams rather than taking the time to pursue yours, you are cheating yourself. You are truly being selfish by not taking the time to cultivate your true gifts with the rest of humanity. The world needs and rewards those who have the courage to develop into who they were meant to be. Go for it.

Find Your True Motives

Do you want to be successful? Why? I'm not being silly here. I had to ask myself these questions, and some of the answers truly surprised me. Think of the movie stars, sports figures, and other celebrities, major and minor, who seemed to have it all and then appeared on the front page of the newspaper, having done something entirely idiotic, sabotaging themselves and their careers and families. Why would these "successful" people throw it all away by committing suicide or becoming drug addicts or criminals? They are typical cases of faulty foundations.

If you want to be successful to "show" your father or your mother, to rub somebody's nose in it, you are building a fifty-story structure on a shaky foundation. Once you arrive, you will feel empty, unsatisfied, and just plain ripped off. When you want to succeed in order to win approval, praise, or love, your motivation is too weak, and the weight of the pressure will tumble it down. It's a simple case of hitting bottom when reaching the top. Let's get totally real. What does success mean to you? Does it mean more money, more time, more things? Second question: would you be happy if you had more of any of those things? Are you happy now?

Let me put it to you simply: You don't reach success and then feel happy. You are happy and *then* reach success. Take a moment, go back, and read that sentence again. Happiness comes first and success follows.

And happiness comes from within. It is not a nebulous concept—hold my hand and let's take it one step at a time. There are several ingredients essential to a symbiotic happiness and success relationship. I'll get you started on my list, and perhaps you would like to add or subtract one or more components to make it yours. Here they are:

Power: Power is the ability and the willingness to act—choosing, deciding, and going for it. You need to feel powerful to feel happy. If you feel like a victim, someone who is not in control of his own life, true happiness is very hard to attain because you are constantly relying on others to provide it. Power is something you take; it is not something you give. Nobody can take your power away unless you give it away. Don't.

Creativity: This is not defined by a label or a career. When you have creativity, you can stimulate free will and thought in yourself and in others. I can't conceive of feeling happy without having the freedom to be creative. This is the ability and willingness to adventure, even if I fail along the way. Failure to me is equivalent to a stop sign on the road. It simply means pause, not give up. You do things and some work, some don't; you do more of the ones that work. It's that simple.

Excellence: Striving for excellence is a vital part of being happy. Excellence means being the best that you can be. It does not imply perfection. In fact, excellence is the opposite of perfection. Excellence means not making success the bull's-eye of your target, not shooting for success but enjoying the means rather than concentrating on the end. To be perfect, you have to be right; to achieve excellence, you need to be willing to be wrong. Perfection is about the destination and excellence about the journey, and if you enjoy the journey, you will enjoy your destination. It's really just taking each moment and living it fully, doing something good and meaningful, one small step at a time. This process diffuses the power of intimidation that the word "success" may hold over you. Successful people are so busy seeking excellence they don't realize they have reached success until someone points it out to them, and then they don't feel any different. Albert Einstein was once asked how he was able to cope with his great reputation. His reply was that he did it by continuing to pursue greater

> *Start by doing what's necessary; then do what's possible; and suddenly you are doing the impossible.*
> —*Saint Francis of Assisi*

goals. He didn't dwell on his successes and kept his mind actively involved in new challenges.

Optimism: This is not just a state of mind or an approach to life. It's a commitment to look for what's working, looking for the good in a situation, and building on that. When you are optimistic and passionate, you actually become more resourceful and creative.

Lessons I Learned Along the Way

Many great inventions are really the product of somebody messing up while trying to do something else. Take 3M, for example. Frustrated that his scrap-paper bookmarks kept falling out of his church choir hymnal, Art Fry, a researcher with the company, used an adhesive that was formerly considered an experiment gone wrong by another scientist at 3M. That was the birth of Post-it Notes. In 1981, one year after their introduction, Post-it Notes were named the company's Outstanding New Product. What this story teaches us is that you don't have to have every detail worked out from the get-go. In fact, the knowing comes simply through the doing. I am not saying that you shouldn't be prepared, trained, and alert. But when preparedness meets opportunity, the process begins to develop and with it the realization of dreams you never even knew you had.

It can happen at any given moment, sometimes when you least expect it. It could be something someone says, a fleeting thought, a feeling, even a smell. Something triggers a response of total resolve that clicks the picture into focus—suddenly you know exactly what step to take next. Follow your instinct, follow that little voice. Chances are the road ahead is your chosen path.

And don't expect it to be fun all the time. Your success will be proportionate to the price you are willing to pay for it and the sacrifices along the way. Nobody says it's going to be easy. What I can assure you, though, is that it will be worth it. Your goal is to work hard but to work joyfully. If you feel the passion for what you do, you will have fun, make money, and make a difference.

> You miss 100 percent of the shots you don't take.
> —Wayne Gretzky

I've been asked, "How do I know my true passion, how do I know if I even have a dream?" You may not be clear or exactly know what that dream is, but it has been etched into your soul. And you are not in it alone. Your intuition, your inner voice, is with you every step of the way, planting clues along the way for you to discover. Pay attention. Be alert.

When you are fearful, you can have problems making decisions and have difficulty overcoming the obstacles that

Julie Stav

are sure to appear along the way. Wanting more is not a bad thing. Setting financial goals is a healthy and positive step toward the realization of your dreams. But concentrating on the gap between what you have and what you want can actually stagnate you. You can honor where you are, appreciate what you have accomplished, and still have dreams and desires.

Celebrate Your Personality

Each personality type has a different idea of what it means to be successful. The important thing is to follow your own definition of success. If you are trying to reach someone else's dreams, you are setting yourself up to fail. Recognize your weaknesses without hiding behind them. Just because you are a logical Diligent Investigator doesn't mean that you should belittle emotions. If you know that empathy does not come easily to you, make the extra effort to incorporate it into your life by taking the time to listen to other people's concerns. Use the knowledge of your weaknesses to conquer them rather than use them to excuse poor behavior. But don't beat yourself up with them either. Celebrating who and what you are today grounds you in good feelings that allow for more of what you are looking for.

If you are experiencing the fear of success, congratulations! It only arises when you are genuinely creating change and moving forward in your life. In other words, you are on to something good! Feel the fear, and then do it anyway. Soon you will be substituting fear with challenge, doubt with conviction, worry with action, inconvenience with growth, discomfort with discovery, and lack of motivation with enthusiasm! You are potentially at the height

> *God does not implant within any human heart a desire which it does not also give the person the ability to fulfill.*
> —*Ralph Waldo Emerson*

of your strength when you are feeling truly vulnerable to failure, when the butterflies are flying in your stomach, your eyes are sparkling, and your gut is the one who's talking, loud and clear.

11

THE
MILLIONAIRE
PERSONALITY

Your personality dictates many things—how you respond to stressful or demanding circumstances, how you interact with yourself and with the world around you. By understanding your personality type, you can enhance the quality of your personal relationships as well as your professional success—it becomes an opportunity to evaluate the parts of yourself you've never paid attention to.

However, even though your temperament is factory-issued, your environment has a great impact on how you handle yourself. The sum total of your life—the positive and negative experiences, the characters who have starred in the drama of your existence—affects the way you manifest your personality.

Regardless of your personality type, your sex, your cultural background, or even your age, you can train yourself to cultivate your strengths to achieve greatness. Yes, no matter what your natural tendencies, your socioeconomic background, or even your level of education, you can use what you already know about yourself as a foundation to build your future, starting today.

Your Very Own Recipe

Let's imagine that you are entertaining and have decided that the main course of the evening will consist of an elegant paella—an elaborate saffron-flavored Spanish dish made with varying combinations of rice, vegetables, meat, chicken, and seafood. You go to your favorite search engine and type in the word "paella." There you found over two million references, each one just a little bit different from the one before! What to do, what to do? Well, you would probably investigate a few of them until you found a satisfying recipe, one that you can customize to your liking. You may opt for the one that calls for the ingredients you may have at hand or that are easily accessible. If you dislike seafood, for example, you will find recipes that concentrate on meats. If you are a vegetarian, chances are you will find one that will use only vegetables. It's your call. And the end result will be paella like no other one, because you made it your way.

Reaching your personal and financial goals works the same way. Your personality traits are the main ingredients in your pantry. But you don't necessarily have to follow one given path to reach your goals. As with the paella, you can choose to add or omit any flavors or textures. It is, after all, *your* paella.

Let's just talk in the context of money for a moment. And let's also assume that your goal is to become "rich." I will leave the definition of the word entirely up to you. Much research has been done to find out which personality has the best "recipe" for achieving wealth. The end result was that the key to richness did not rest in any one particular personality type. Instead, the secret passage to fortune (and sometimes fame) was reached by those who deciphered the codes of their own personalities and used their strengths to propel them to success.

Yes, they all had their weaknesses, but the rich, the millionaires, have learned to be aware of their counterproductive traits and utilize them as warning signs to avoid the pot holes along the way. They chose the ingredients for their paella very carefully. Do you want to know how they did it? Here is a list of the staple ingredients they kept in their pantry:

A glass half full: There is no question about it: Winners accentuate the positive. Instead of allowing themselves to quit based on any setbacks along the way, they see opportunities to learn and grow. They are uncritical of themselves when they make a mistake, and they use their energies to prepare for each day by arming themselves with mental tools that allow them to handle adversity. They are honest with themselves and learn from their mistakes. If they get off course, they recover swiftly.

A master plan: They may not have every detail of their future mapped out, but winners do have some sense of the steps ahead. Their course of action is a work in progress that is streamlined along the way with persistence and resolve.

An urge to earn it: The millionaires truly feel good about money. They feel there is enough to go around in the universe, and they do not feel guilty if they have more than someone else. Self-made millionaires feel justified and worthy in their use of money. If you hold a mental picture of a millionaire as someone who is scrambling to gobble more of the pie at the expense of others, you are definitely not thinking like one.

A belief in investing: The millionaires invest between 15 and 20 percent of their household income every year. Millionaires who have made their own fortunes are typically more aggressive in their investments than those who inherited their money. They understand that the secret to making money in the stock market is to make more money than you lose.

A meaningful project: A millionaire mind-set finds ways to turn talents and passions into a lucrative endeavor. It's amazing to see how many people try to find fortunes in faraway places while they overlook obvious opportunities to succeed in their own backyard, doing what they enjoy most.

A group of unequivocal friends: Millionaires engage in relationships with people who believe in them. That doesn't mean that they don't interact with all kinds of people, even the negative ones, but they keep them in perspective, not allowing the unbelievers to sabotage them.

A knowledge that they could do it all over again: Millionaires are people who like to work and they are confident in their ability to make money. It is not unusual to find that most millionaires have failed at a prior business. They see money and success as a process that needs to be tended and not as a stagnated pool that needs to be preserved.

How can knowing your own personality traits and those of the people around you help you become rich? By enabling you to realize which of your natural tendencies help you and which could make you stumble.

For example, if you are a Do-Gooder, you may feel overly responsible and loyal to the team, perhaps even at your own expense. You may need to set limits for yourself and others in your contributions to the tribe. Or you may opt for investments that meet the high standards of your soul but fall short on performance. Attempt to find the balance between these two.

If you are a very detail-oriented person, a Diligent Investigator, you may become so lost in the details that you miss key leverage points. You may also be so tired by the minutiae that you simply run out of steam before arriving at a decision that could have proven very fruitful. You may set a time limit or shorten the list of conditions to help you decide on a course of action. Remember that you will never know *everything* about *anything*.

You may be a Diva, very capable of not only taking care of yourself, but actually of becoming very rich on your own. But the thought of being alone for the rest of your life could be so overwhelming that you end up sabotaging yourself subconsciously, remaining in a "waiting room" until you find Mr. Right, because down deep you feel you need a man to be rich and you don't think you can make it on your own. It's amazing how many successful, highly educated career women share this self-destructive fantasy.

Or how about our optimist Dionysian? Your spending plan may find the balance it craves just by simply substituting the statement "I don't make enough money" with "I spend more money than I make." The first statement paints you as a victim of your circumstances while the second one puts you in complete control of your free will. It really boils down to taking control and taking responsibility. It's as simple as that.

The Violinist

This is the story of a very poor and defeated violinist who would stand on the sidewalk of one of the streets in Paris to play his old violin. The unkempt man would place his beret on the ground in front of him in the hope that some of the passersby would take pity and would deposit some coins in the crumpled headdress.

The poor man tried in vain to squeeze a melody out of his untamed instrument. But instead, all he managed to produce was a monotonous and unidentifiable series of sounds that screeched through the air and made him sound more like a car alarm than a musician.

One day, a very gifted and famous violinist happened to walk by with a group of friends. He wrinkled his face in horror, insulted by the sacrilegious performance of the man. He took a look at the couple of coins that rested in the beret, asked for the violin, and proceeded to fine-tune it. Then, with the vigor of a true master, he transformed the sad-looking contraption into the magical instrument it was meant to be. His friends began to applaud, and before long, a crowd gathered around to listen to the strange concerto. Soon thereafter, the beret began to fill up with not only coins, but bills of all denominations, as the master continued to play one and then another melody, each more beautiful than the one before.

The lesser musician's eyes were gleaming! He couldn't believe his luck! As the money poured into his hat, he jumped up and down in delight as he yelled to the crowd: "That's my violin! He's playing my violin!" Which, of course, was true.

We were all born with a violin. It represents your mental capacity, your attitude, and your personality. It is up to you how you will play it. Some of you may choose not to fine-tune it. You may not be willing to study, learn, and sharpen your skills in order to play it like a master. And yet, you may expect your hat to be filled with money while you play a dissonant song.

You may feel that the world owes you a living or that those who succeed are just plain lucky. And that couldn't be farther from the truth. You may think you know your rights, but you feel no sense of obligation to earn them. But some of you know that we need to learn sooner or later that the best comes to those who not only fine-tune their violin, but also learn to play it masterfully over time.

The Herd Mentality

Up until the year 1954, the general consensus was that it was well beyond human ability to run one mile in less than four minutes. Most people did not dispute this widely known fact. That is, until May 6 of that year, when a young medical student accomplished the impossible. Roger Bannister ran a mile in three minutes and fifty-nine-point-four seconds. Roger had broken more than the world's record for the mile run. He had destroyed the myth that such a thing couldn't actually be achieved. Since that fateful day, the record for that distance has been broken several times, and it now stands at just a fraction above three minutes and forty-three seconds by a man from Morocco named Hicham El Guerrouj.

How could a record that was considered to be insurmountable be broken? *Because someone believed that it could.* Roger was willing to believe in himself, in spite of the general opinion shared by others. What do you *believe* that you can accomplish? If you don't have a clear picture in your mind, perhaps you have been spinning in place on automatic pilot. It's time you fine-tune your violin.

Are you surrounded by positive people; do you know who your biggest fans are? Or do you see yourself having to make excuses for your own successes just so you don't make someone dear to you feel inferior? Good intentions, bad habit—and a mark of less than stellar self-esteem. Your self-esteem is an automatic, instant picture you have taken of who you think you are based on the result of your past experiences. High self-esteem is the best vaccine against distress, depression, helplessness, and dependency.

If you have been successful in playing tennis, you probably like to play, which would make you better at it; eventually you will come to believe that you are a pretty decent tennis player. See how you arrive at that conclusion? If you have engaged in successful investing, you have probably made some money, which made you invest more money still. That improved your ability to make money, and you probably consider yourself a good investor. These good experiences help to buttress and buoy your overall picture of yourself, creating a surplus of positive self-esteem in your inner account—handy for those times when a debit threatens to snatch some of that good stuff from you.

Maybe you are late to a meeting, you may get a flat tire on your way to work, or you may lose money in the stock market. When that happens, you go to your self-esteem reserves to find relief. If it's full, you can recover quickly. In fact, you can even reframe what happened in such a way that, instead of emptying the contents of your self-esteem account, it adds to it.

If, on the other hand, you find an empty account, you

may find yourself shifting into survival mode—resorting to your most primitive and ingrained instincts. At this point many will surrender to that inner critical voice and the facets of their personality that work against them.

The shift takes fractions of a second. You can go from feeling scared to feeling powerful, from feeling out of control to knowing that you, and only you, are judge and jury of your existence and the choices you make. But there is a quick fix and a feeling of relief when you get in the old pattern, even if it ultimately works against you.

Give Me Some Self-Esteem!

Here again, the good news–bad news dilemma exists. The bad news is that I can't give you self-esteem. You, however, can take it. It all starts with you thinking about something that made you feel good about yourself. I don't care how far back you have to go. Think about it and smile to yourself. If you can't think of anything, don't worry. You can borrow it from somebody else. This is what a mentor is—a person whom you can emulate until you can adopt his or her qualities as your own. Pretty good, eh?

Mentors can come in so many different forms; you don't even have to know them personally to be able to draw from *their* account. Did you realize that? Your mentor can be an athlete you admire, a teacher you had when you were eight years old, a parent, an uncle, a friend, even a fictional character. Give yourself a mentor and have frequent conversations with her. When you have a problem or you get that funny feeling in the pit of your stomach that is telling you that something is not right, or you don't know what to do, go to the mentor in your mind and ask yourself, "How would X respond to this?"

I've had many mentors throughout my life. One of them was Don Quixote de la Mancha. This person doesn't even exist, other than as a figment of the imagination of Miguel de Cervantes y Saavedra in his essential novel of the same name. But to me, he was very real indeed. As a matter of fact, whenever I felt down, scared, or just plain bored, I would sing the song "Man of La Mancha" to myself and feel an immediate sense of power and vitality. That song replenished my account.

You have all the ingredients you need to shape the course of your life. They're there, inside of you, patiently waiting for you to discover them and fine-tune them. I hope you come to visit me at www.juliestav.com and share your experiences with me as you get to know yourself for the work of art you truly are.